over my

shoulder

Tales of Life, Death and Almost Everything In Between

Azalea Art Press
Southern Pines, North Carolina

ISBN: 978-1-943471-03-4

for bruce and beth

contents

What (cont.)

Where

When

Why

Foreword

Writing a book has been in the back of my mind for several years. I was enjoying a freelance career with many media outlets during the 50 or so years I've been writing for publication. Quite by chance, I was looking for a column from several years ago and when I read it I thought that it stood the test of time. Thus began a journey through scrapbooks and files leading to this collection.

There is no world-shattering theme to these columns. I have made no attempt to place them in chronological order. They are loosely grouped according the 'Five W's' every newsperson has emblazoned in her memory: Who, What, Where, When and Why.

The year a column or article was printed is included to provide reference for the reader. I have jumped around according to topic rather than date. There are some years not represented. As I have been a hard news reporter, a newsletter editor, a feature writer and columnist, there have been some years when only hard news was on the agenda. In many cases it was local news, which is now quite out of date and not relevant.

My first career was teaching. When my family started to move around, I slipped into the newsroom instead of the classroom. There have been two people with whom I worked in those early days who have greatly influenced me. Reverend Tom Raby of the Kingston office of The Canadian Register, a national Catholic Weekly in Canada, and Jack Wood, Oswego bureau chief for the Syracuse newspapers. Father Tom taught me the value of humor and humanity in columns. Jack imparted the need for getting the story, getting it right and getting it before deadline. Both are no longer with us, but I am forever grateful.

What I've tried to do in this collection is tell interesting tales. Some happened to my family and me. Many could have happened to anyone. It is my hope that you will have a few "aha" moments, some smiles or chuckles or perhaps a few tears.

- Ann Murphy Robson
September 2015

Introduction

The first time I met Ann Robson was at my office at OutreachNC magazine in Southern Pines, North Carolina in mid-2010. We had just launched our monthly magazine, which is geared for baby boomers. Ann had come by to meet this then thirty-something kid of an editor, who was feeling her way through the first few issues of a brand new endeavor.

Ann came prepared with sample columns and ideas, including caregiving tips, since many readers are sandwiched between their own families and aging parents. It was a conversation that became easier as it progressed and grew into a friendship.

Ann began submitting columns on a variety of topics related to the demographic, offering story ideas and taking on feature articles as issues turned into years of publication.

A year later, when I struggled for a gift idea for Ann, I remembered her mentioning that she and other lefties read magazines from the back to the front. In that spirit, I offered her the magazine's inside left back page for her "Over My Shoulder" column. I considered Ann as this editor's "Andy Rooney" with her quick wit and lessons learned through a personal story.

Over her tenure, she has written about friends, family, her beloved Canada, her Irish roots and life's journey. Perhaps our most memorable moment was the opportunity to do something Ann had placed on her bucket list (or 'life list' as she prefers to call it) — for a hot air balloon ride. I scheduled an interview with a retired pilot turned hot air balloonist, helping Ann mark something off her life list in celebration of a milestone birthday and as a thank you for her contributions to the magazine. It seemed to be the perfect present. The only caveat being that it was a sunrise takeoff for her non-morning personality. Forgiving me for the o-dark-thirty hour, Ann wholeheartedly accepted.

As I peppered the balloonist with questions and took furious notes, Ann and our photographer, Diana Matthews, climbed into the basket and anticipated their ride. The basket literally floated up, up and away into a beautiful Carolina blue sky, and Ann never stopped smiling.

As you read these collected works of my writer friend, there will be moments of laughter, advice to ponder and put to use and tales of her own adventures. Ann's tidbits of wisdom were a reader favorite for OutreachNC, and I can assure you that the words within the pages ahead will offer the same smiles and inspiration.

- Carrie Frye
Editor
OutreachNC

who

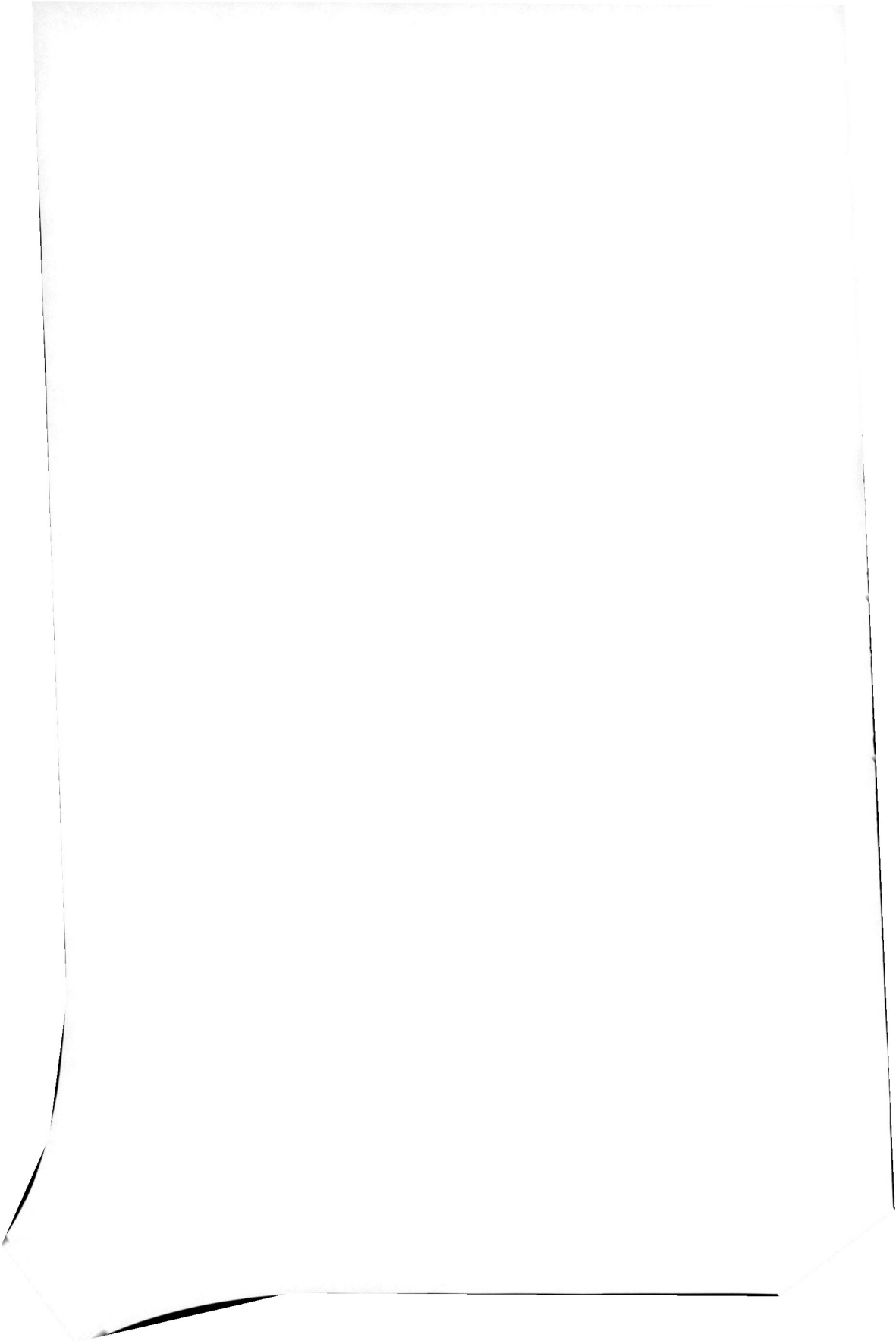

Immigrant

June, 2006

I am an immigrant.

I came into the United States in April 1968, green card in hand. We came from the northern border after months of following the legal steps mandated by the Immigration and Naturalization Service. Fourteen years later we chose to become United States citizens. That process took longer than getting our green cards but we followed the rules.

As law-abiding Canadians it never occurred to us to slip across the border posing as Northern tourists seeking warmer weather. I've often commented to friends who were born in this country that if the average person on the street who is a proud American had to jump through some of the INS hoops, they might not get that precious piece of paper, which declares that you are a citizen of The United States of America.

One of the first steps we had to take was getting fingerprinted at our local police station. Those prints were then thoroughly checked by several police agencies, including the beloved Royal Canadian Mounted Police. We cleared that hurdle. Next there was lots of paperwork, which we carefully completed, knowing that a wrong answer could delay or deny our being able to move to West Virginia where my husband's international company thought he should go.

Our house, our very first house which we had owned less than a year, was put on the market. A deal was made and a closing date set. Movers were contacted. As the day drew closer we weren't confident that our green cards would arrive in time. We were told we had to go to Montreal for a final, final interview, and a medical exam.

We were to bring chest x-rays with us to prove we did not have TB.

The Montreal part of the process annoyed me the most. We were treated like cattle and visions of immigrants going through Ellis Island kept flashing before me. The medical exam was perfunctory but profitable for the doctor. We had to repeat verbally things we had written on our applications. (Oh, I know they were just double-checking but in my late 20s I wasn't sure why any of this "stuff" had to be done.)

For years we had been welcomed as tourists spending money up and down the Atlantic seaboard. But, aha! Now we were going to actually live here. We were going to be part of the system. We got Social Security cards, tax forms, a new bank account, and a Sears' credit card. We were also paying taxes contributing to the economy more generously than we had as occasional visitors.

It was close, but the green cards arrived in time for us to leave as planned. Having crossed at the Thousand Islands/Ivy Lea border point many times, I didn't feel any real turmoil about leaving my native land and starting a new and different life. As it happened, we were making that very same crossing around noon on September 11, 2001, having just learned about the attacks on the World Trade Center.

Word had gotten out that the border crossings were to be closed but they were open. Not many people were crossing into New York that day. Many were heading into Canada, particularly truck drivers caught in limbo. As we pulled away from the second span of the Thousand Islands Bridge and saw the sign "Welcome to New York," my eyes filled with tears. I knew then that I was an American. Thugs had attacked us as well as the rest of the country.

As beautiful and wonderful as West Virginia can be, I don't think that should be the first impression of "life in America" for two people who grew up in a lovely cosmopolitan capital city.

Naively, I didn't think there'd be much of an adjustment. Canadians and Americans pretty well spoke the same language, shared a lot of popular culture, so what could be so bad? But until we became citizens 14 years later, we were "resident aliens" who had to report our whereabouts annually to local authorities.

Canadians *are* different from Americans. We don't have a simple explanation of what it is to be Canadian but many Canadians will answer they're not Americans when asked to define themselves. Our differences lie, as do most things, in our histories. We broke away from England rather peacefully in 1867 after serious discussions about how to conduct ourselves as a new confederation. The American separation from Mother England was hardly peaceful.

The United States is known worldwide as 'the great melting pot' where people from different nations come together and assimilate into a large American family. At least that's the theory. Canada uses 'the vertical mosaic' model, which allows for various ethnic, social, religious groups to clump together, retain many of their customs, and live happily ever after as part of Canada. Another theory.

There is no perfect way to bring in new citizens and make them part of the fabric of a country. The situation we now find ourselves in concerning laws for illegal immigrants, proposals for alleviating the situation, and trying to reconcile all sides of the question proves that the melting pot doesn't appear to work anymore.

It's difficult to point fingers and correct a decades old problem. The first person to hire an illegal immigrant and look the other way so he wouldn't have to pay a fair wage is the real culprit. Now we say we need immigrant workers to do labor that Americans won't do. If we need them, then let them come here legally. For those already here as productive members of American society we need to find a solution that is fair. Rewarding law breaking does not seem to me to be fair. Those who help bring illegal immigrants here should be severely penalized. Those who hire them without documentation also should be penalized.

Since Congress took the easy out and left Washington for a couple of weeks, I have little hope that anything substantive will come from any compromise bill quilted together in an election year and hovered over by those whose interests do not include words like "legal" and "fair."

I am a proud, legal immigrant who became a citizen and flies the American flag daily and only occasionally raises the Canadian one beneath it to welcome Canadian visitors or celebrate a Canadian holiday.

My wish would be that those millions of immigrants floating between deportation and legality will one day be able to proudly proclaim themselves as legal residents, soon-to-be citizens.

an irish blessing *March, 1986*

With a family heritage that includes such names as Murphy, O'Meara, Ryan, O'Brien, Houlihan, Finnerty and the like, you can imagine that St. Patrick's Day has always been well celebrated by me and mine.

Sixteen years ago today we got our best Irish blessing. Our daughter Beth arrived in the final hour of the day. I should have realized that she was making a statement, even then. She was a few weeks early but chose to keep us in suspense until the last minute as to whether she'd make it in time to be an official St. Patrick's Day leprechaun. She still chooses to do things in her own time and still manages to keep us in suspense.

A child's 16th birthday gives a parent cause to stop and wonder where those years have gone and to reflect on the highs and lows. We feel very fortunate that there have been many more highs than lows in the past 16 years. That is not to imply that it has been smooth sailing every day.

There were days when I wondered if this little bundle of joy would make it through childhood. During the first six years of her life we became well acquainted with the emergency room procedures. First there were stitches in her chin, then in her forehead, then near her eye. We weren't abusive parents. She was adventurous and accident prone. Then there was a broken leg followed by sprains and dislocations in various areas. There were many days when I wondered if I'd make it through her childhood.

First steps, first words, firsts of any kind are monumental occasions. I remember being elated the first time she put a logical thought together and verbalized what she was thinking. How did I know this verbal, logical trait would come to be dreaded by me in later years when I was trying to enforce discipline or something equally foolish that parents try to do?

During her early years we lived in a rural setting with a river in our backyard. Watching the ever-changing seasons and landscape through fresh, bright new eyes brought a whole new meaning to trees, and water, and birds, and fish, and sunsets, and even thunderstorms.

We had always liked to travel and decided that a third person in the family wasn't going to slow us down. So, at six weeks, we took her to a wedding in Philadelphia and it seems we've been on the go ever since. Now she can claim to have been in all but 10 of our 50 states.

In these 16 years we've moved twice. The first was the more traumatic as it was her first move after 13 years in the place where she was born. The second was two years later. Both times she was a big help in the transition. We are proud of the way she has adapted to different situations and feel comfortable that this skill will help her the rest of her life.

Before our second move, we were interviewed by a psychologist whose specialty is teens. She has an interesting radio program on NPR in Cleveland. She questioned my sanity about moving a teenager. I replied that Beth was an OK kid. The doctor then said I was the first parent of a teenager to come to her program and have positive things to say about the family teen. My reply was that I'd said she was OK, but not perfect. She is OK. Most days, she's a whole lot more than OK—but then I'm prejudiced because she's our Irish blessing.

leprechauns *March, 1975*

We have four leprechauns at our house.

I come from a long line of Irish folk, so my belief in these Irish elves is not unusual.

Three of our leprechauns have been in the family for years. You can find them in the garden in summer and adding a warm, magical touch to our hearth in winter. The fourth one arrived on St. Patrick's Day, 1970 and if ever there was a magical creature, she's it.

Leprechauns are noted for their impish nature, appearing here and there but never really seen. Legends attribute different characteristics to them. The most popular myth is that if you can catch a leprechaun he'll show you where to find the pot o' gold at the end of the rainbow.

Our very own leprechaun has brought both the gold and the rainbow to our lives. She brightens dull days with her happy chatter. Her smiles, hugs and kisses are worth more to us than several pots filled with gold.

Beth's Murphy grandparents had waited ten years for a grandchild and were elated with the timing of her arrival. It's hard to believe that five years have escaped since then. I suppose every parent feels that way many times during a child's life—where had the time gone? When did she turn from helpless babe into delightful little girl?

I've often commented, sometimes seriously, sometimes in jest, that if we knew in advance what parenthood had to offer, there'd be fewer parents around. As I watched her get stitches in her chin at two, her forehead at three, and a leg cast at four, I couldn't help but think that Dr. Spock hadn't warned me enough.

As any parent will admit, the precious moments that happen only once and escape forever are what make it all worthwhile. The special hug for no reason other than "I love you, Mom and Dad" or the thoughtful sharing of a favorite Raggedy Andy doll "to make you feel better, Mom" when you have a miserable headache and would like to crawl into a cave.

Some of you still may not believe in leprechauns, thinking me daft for admitting their very existence. I can't help it, you see—every morning I'm greeted by the dark, twinkling eyes of a St. Patrick's Day child who is filled with the impish spirit attributed to those Irish legendary creatures.

Among other things celebrated in February, it's "Spunky Old Broads" month.

Finally! Some recognition for those women who have reached a certain age and maintain an enthusiastic outlook on life. For some outstanding women, "broad" may not be the best word but it takes nothing away from the very nature of the woman, rather it provides a description of a person of strong will, often with a very good sense of humor thrown in.

Gayle Carson, 72, three-time cancer survivor, psychiatrist and talk show host, started the Spunky Old Broads movement with a couple of friends over a cup of coffee. Their philosophy has become: Loving life has become a habit for me, so it looks easy and, it can become a habit for you.

They're all around us, these spunky old broads. We may not recognize them because to those who don't understand, or appreciate the term, they just don't seem to fit in.

Probably the most outstanding spunky old broad of our era was Betty Friedan who literally opened doors and windows for women encouraging them to be themselves and help others to do the same. I met Ms. Friedan in the 70s when she was on a book tour for "The Feminine Mystique." At a press conference following her reading, she was a gracious host taking many questions, never making fun of the stupid questions, always grateful for the intelligent ones.

In Kentucky I met two spunky old broads who loved art and literature, Joy Bale Boone and Mary Ellen Miller. They drew me in and in a few short years, between us we helped establish a Canadian Studies program at Western Kentucky University, and then followed that with our greatest achievement—the Center for Robert Penn Warren Studies. I believe Joy knew almost everyone in Kentucky and knew whom to ask for help in whatever project. Mary Ellen was employed by the University so had some limits on her activity. But that didn't mean that she couldn't point her friends to this project or that seminar and those spunky old broad friends would see that things got done. Joy was named Poet Laureate of Kentucky and brought her love of poetry to every nook and cranny of the state. (There was a great trip to Paris, but that's a whole other story. Suffice to say that three Spunky Old Broads from Kentucky held their own in Paris.)

We have some great "broads" among us in the area:

Ellen Airs is a charming, vocal advocate for NAMI, Habitat, and anything that will help someone else. She's also a lot of fun and a joy to have as a friend. (I don't think she qualifies for the 'old' part of spunky broads, but I've never asked.)

Another is the apparently meekest, sweetest lady, Mary Crusius. She is spunky, she has crossed the 'old' threshold, but she's probably more of a lady. She didn't amass her cache of Senior Olympic medals by not having that extra portion of 'spunk' to get her over the finish line, over the hurdles, and wiping the court with tennis opponents.

Beth Takahashi is another broad/lady hybrid and her life story proves the 'spunky' part.

When, or if, I ever really grow up, I want to have parts of all these ladies as part of me.

beautiful women *January, 2011*

Much to my surprise, I have learned that this is Beautiful Women Month. E-mail messages from separate educators in Michigan, both of them beautiful women, have advised me of this special month. I hasten to point out this has nothing to do with "beauty" as perceived by the general public. Instead, it is a celebration of women whose inner beauty and depth of character enrich our lives. Look around. You are probably looking at more than one beautiful woman and had not thought about what made her special.

To all the beautiful women I know—hope this makes you smile. The following was written by Audrey Hepburn who was asked to share "beauty tips":

> For attractive lips, speak words of kindness.
> For lovely eyes, seek out the good in people.
> For a slim figure, share your food with the hungry.
> For beautiful hair, let a child run his or her fingers through it once a day.
> For poise, walk with the knowledge that you never walk alone.
> People, even more than things, have to be restored, renewed, revived, reclaimed and redeemed; never throw out anyone.
> Remember, if you ever need a helping hand, you'll find one at the end of each of your arms. As you grow older, you will discover that you have two hands, one for helping yourself, the other for helping others.

The beauty of a woman is not in the clothes she wears, the figure that she carries, or the way she combs her hair. The beauty of a woman must be seen from in her eyes, because that is the doorway to her heart, the place where love resides.
The beauty of a woman is not in a facial mode, but the true beauty in a woman is reflected in her soul. It is the caring that she lovingly gives the passion that she shows.
The beauty of a woman grows with the passing years.
(Now that's something I can identify with!)

Some hard facts about women:

The average woman weighs 144 lbs. and wears between a 12-14.
One out of every four college aged women has an eating disorder.
The models in the magazines are airbrushed—not perfect!
A psychological study in 1995 found that three minutes spent looking at a fashion magazine caused 70 percent of women to feel depressed, guilty and shameful.
Models twenty years ago weighed 8% less than the average woman. Today they weigh 23% less.

An English professor wrote the words, "Woman without her man is nothing," on the blackboard and directed the students to punctuate it correctly. The men wrote: "Woman, without her man, is nothing." The women wrote: "Woman! Without her, man is nothing."

The Images of Mother:

4 years of age—My Mommy can do anything!
8 years of age—My Mom knows a lot! A whole lot!
12 years of age—My Mother doesn't really know quite everything.
14 years of age—Naturally, Mother doesn't know that, either.
16 years of age—Mother? She's hopelessly old-fashioned.
18 years of age—That old woman? She's way out of date!
25 years of age—Well, she might know a little bit about it.
35 years of age—Before we decide, let's get Mom's opinion.
45 years of age—Wonder what Mom would have thought about it?
65 years of age—Wish I could talk it over with Mom.

Be sure to thank at least one beautiful woman for her effect on your life.

Mothers: Our Model for Caregivers

April, 2010

Mothers are the first caregivers in our lives. After giving birth to us, they nourish us, clothe us, keep us safe, teach us, and most of all, love us.

Every child with a scraped knee runs quickly to her mother who will 'kiss it and make it better.' As scraped knees give way to crushing disappointments or to broken hearts, mothers are still needed to try and make it better. The mother's kiss and touch help soothe whatever hurt we may encounter, at whatever age.

We learn from these caring women how to care for others. Sometimes, the tables get turned on us and we become the caregiver for our mothers, thus becoming our 'mother's mother.' Grown children find this a tough role to accept. They are used to being helped by their mothers, counting on them for love, support and guidance throughout the years.

As hard as it is to assume caring for your parents, it's not easy for them either. They are used to being the head and heart of the family and aren't sure why roles have reversed. How many times have you heard a mother say, "I don't want to be a burden to my children?" Yet, they never felt that you were a burden to them when you kept them up at night with colic or teething, or when you were a teenager who may have stayed out late knowing that when you came home, Mom would be waiting. Mothers didn't mind those late night calls that disturbed their well earned rest just as long as we were all right and just needed to check in.

Many of us feel awkward when our mothers need help with personal care and daily living. Remembering that they once held our soiled bodies in their tender hands can help us see the circle of care that goes on. We may experience sadness and frustration seeing that once vital individual changed by disease. Our mothers have been our strength. Now it's our turn to show them your lessons were well learned.

I used to use the phrase "where is it written that mothers have to . . ." One day my daughter stopped me dead in my tracks when she was about 5 or 6 saying that it was written on page 264 of the Mothers' Manual! Although such a manual did not physically exist, I must have made her believe there was such a magic book someplace.

I'm sure that despite what I know about caregiving, that I'll likely say to her, "where is it written that you have to take care of me?" if that time comes. I know that she'll have a quick, sensible answer and likely quote me. I've done a lot speaking and teaching on this subject so my words may well come back to save me.

lifelong *May, 2002*

We come in all shapes and sizes.
We come in different colors.
We have different views and temperaments.
We learn on the job.
We are with you from cradle to grave.
We feed and clothe you.
We laugh at your antics. Sometimes we have to frown.
We take care of bumps, bruises, and broken hearts.
We hope and pray that nothing more serious happens to you.
We are proud of you most of the time. Other times, we may be embarrassed.
We sing to you, read to you, play games with you.
We are chauffeurs, nurses, doctors, psychologists, mediators and consultants.
We are your moral compass.
We can be disciplinarians, but always "for your own good."
We are your friend, companion, cheerleader.
We learn to understand sports so we can cheer at the right times, never yell at the coaches, referees, other players and their parents.
We try not to embarrass with our enthusiasm but sometimes get carried away, knowing that, no matter what, you have an angel on your shoulder who really loves you.
We are the source of all knowledge until you discover television and computers.

We are grateful for your help with TV remotes, cell phones and computers so we can appear somewhat 'hip' in this new age.
We have big shoulders to cry or lean on.
We occasionally have blinders and may miss something important. If you have to, take the blinders off for us.
We know that some of us weren't cut out for this job and you may suffer sometimes. Find someone with a warm heart to fill in the gaps.
We read to you and treasure those precious moments laughing at *The Cat in the Hat.*
We teach you to drive, to cook, to do laundry, to clean your room and other basics of life. We know you won't always be living in the same house as us so we try to get you ready to leave the nest.
We leave the 'Welcome' sign out for you to come home at any time, for any reason.
We hope that as we age you'll remember some of the things we need.
We love you to the end of the earth and back.
We are your Mothers and Grandmothers.

real men

May, 1982

Note: It was a slow news week when this appeared across the bottom half of the front page of The Oswego Valley News. Reader reaction was pro and con and plentiful.

An insignificant looking paperback has been on the bestseller list for two weeks now. Titled "Real Men Don't Eat Quiche" with a subtitle "A Guidebook to All That is Truly Masculine," this 93-page compilation of essays stretched into a paperback is making waves.

My brother introduced us to it. He and my husband seized on the "real men" phrase as did the rest of us in the family who happen to be "real women," unless you count the five-year old twin boys who are real men in training. None of us would argue that they are not real men. However, they may lose their A-1 standing in that club when it is revealed that they both eat quiche.

My brother is married to a fabulous cook and would be a fool not to eat anything she prepares. He does proclaim his real man status by smothering some things with ketchup or hot sauce just so no one knows he does enjoy food that real men are not supposed to consume.

My husband, on the other hand, is married to a less than fabulous cook, but knows that if quiche is presented to him, he has two choices: *eat it or wear it.* Since real men would never wear quiche, this real man will eat it.

There are a lot of things that author Bruce Feinstein says real men do and don't do. Having seen him on Phil Donahue show, I now have serious doubts about Feinstein's credibility. He did admit that the whole thing started as tongue-in-cheek and, if read that way, the book is a lot of fun.

What bothers me about it is, that after years of breaking down barriers between male and female, in one moment of levity this book starts to draw lines again. Several reporters and book reviewers have written responses to Feinstein. So now we have "real men" and "real women" reigniting the debate between the sexes once again.

Feinstein's litany of credentials for "real men" includes: they don't disco; don't eat brunch; don't have their hair styled; don't itemize tax deductions; they do pass in the no-passing zones; eat meat and potatoes; don't know how to cook but do know how to thaw.

He has devoted one page to his version of "real women." We don't drive as well as real men; we have no past we'll tell you about; we do not believe in palimony; don't major in sociology; we are not afraid to eat quiche which we no doubt have cooked.

The danger with lists is that you are likely to leave something out. Feinstein certainly has. Even if he's only joking, he needs to know that his list is neither accurate nor complete. To add to his lists, I submit:

> Real men don't care who eats what, as long as they get something to eat such as a home cooked meal now and then.
>
> Real women, on the other hand, don't mind serving that meal but would like some friendly conversation with it.
>
> Real men admit to watching "Dallas" or the soaps.
>
> Real women admit to watching "Monday Night Football."

Real men check the oil, water, tires and all that sort of stuff considered necessary to keep a woman's car operational.

Real women know that it is easier to let a real man fix a tire than it is for a real woman to fix a bruised ego.

Real men don't laugh out loud when real women tell them the car has a funny squeak and shouldn't he check it out.

Real women stand their ground in the face of condescending service men and make them fix the car or the stove or the washing machine or whatever, or else real women won't pay the bill.

Real men share household chores, but don't wear aprons.

Real women let them help around the house and don't criticize, nag, make suggestions or do it over.

Real men love kids. So do real women.

Real men are proud of their real women whether they are local reporters or president of IBM.

Real women appreciate that pride.

Real men are not threatened by real women.

Real women aren't threatened by real men.

Real men would be better off spending the cost of Feinstein's book on flowers for a real woman.

Generations *June, 1976*

For almost seven years I lived across from a charming gentleman who was the father of a large family, a grandfather and great-grandfather. He did all is own outside work and took care of his house. He lived alone but was surrounded by family of more than one generation. I had been told that among his many accomplishments he liked to write poetry. Several people had suggested him as a subject for this column (Spotlight.)

I don't know why I didn't get around to it sooner. I always intended to. This spring, time ran out for Fred Loughrey. Although somewhat late, I'm finally featuring him. Before he died, Fred wrote a tribute to his family titled "Rich But Not in Gold" for them to open when he died. The family has graciously consented to share that with us to use as our Fathers' Day tribute.

Rich But Not in Gold

My dear wife, Eunice, with the help of the Good Lord, blessed me with one of the greatest families in the world. I love each and every one, barring none.

To be possessed with a gift like this, all the money in world cannot buy. So I am one of the richest men in the world, thanks to the Good Lord.

We are all borned to live and we live to die and death will not pass one of us by.

So now that I am gone, please do not weep or cry or be sad at heart because I am just another old man that had to depart.

The Good Lord has His ways of softening you up so you don't mind when you depart.

When you are sad at heart please think of me because when you are sad, I am sad too.

So let me have a peaceful rest because I am always with you in life as well as death.

Dad
Fred L. Loughery,
I love you all.

Fathers *June, 2012*

This month we celebrate fathers. It seems that with graduations and weddings, fathers get short shrift on their day. Perhaps that's just because that's the way they are—taking care of their families in an understated way that says, "Don't make a fuss."

They are a somewhat taken for granted breed. Most of them were brought up in traditional households where their mothers stayed home, took care of the kids, did the household chores and appeared to do so effortlessly. Dad went to work to financially provide for his family. He usually did outside chores like mowing the grass, painting the house, checking the roof, clearing the gutters, keeping the family car running.

A lot has changed for men, particularly those who have retired. Suddenly they have a spouse who can no longer do daily chores. She may have a temporary situation or a chronic one. In any case, she is now the one needing help.

Not many men expected that one day they would be a caregiver. They have not been taught the intricacies of today's washing machine with all its choices and electronic controls. They are a little more friendly with a microwave oven but not without some challenges. A vacuum cleaner seems like a reasonably user-friendly appliance but modern technology has "improved" our lives so much that we spend half the time figuring out the instructions and then are so frustrated that we don't feel like seeing if it really works on all surfaces, if the attachments work or if the house is cleaner than when you started.

Making a meal is a big problem. One very intelligent man in one of my caregiver classes had a wonderful plan to make his wife's special recipe. It had a number of ingredients and he checked his list. About halfway through he discovered he was missing an ingredient. It was near the bottom of the recipe and if he had called any of the women in the class, she could have given him advice for a substitute. His wife had Alzheimer's disease and couldn't help him. He was heartbroken that he couldn't carry through his grand plan. He did eventually call one of his daughters and was able to get dinner ready, even though it was not the one he planned.

In a different class, another man took a novel approach. The first day of class he announced that what he would like from his classmates was "recipes!" By the end of the six weeks we had a mini-recipe exchange going and we all benefitted.

One of the more difficult tasks for the male caregiver is the routine of daily life—bathing, dressing, toileting, eating. It seems to be a tough thing for a son or husband to bathe and dress his mother, grandmother or spouse.

We tend to think that men take care of all the financial household matters when, in fact, many women do this. It's an important chore for both before it's too late. Share the information about monthly bills and statements, insurance companies, investments, legal documents.

Women have typically been the ones to remember birthdays, anniversaries and family events. Make a list while you can.

To help the next generation, women should make sure that her spouse knows how to do more than pick up his socks and boil water. We should have taught those years ago but it's not too late. Being a caregiver is not easy for anyone. Men seem to have a more difficult time because so many things are unknown to them.

baby boomers *September, 2000*

I'm finally beginning to appreciate the Baby Boom generation. I'm rethinking my position on the self-centered conspicuous consumers for whom I've had little use in the past.

But, Mother Nature, bless her, is catching up with them. They are beginning to age! They may not like it much but it's something that, if we're lucky, happens to all of us.

What pleases me about *their* aging is that there are so many of them. They are a force to be reckoned with and they're not used to sitting idly by and letting the world pass them by. Now their attention is shifting to what is going to happen to them in this coming stage of their lives.

They will not settle for inferior health care, poor housing for seniors, and inadequate training for professional caregivers. They know how to get things done and they're not about to stop now.

They find themselves faced with an ever-changing family picture of blended families, stepfamilies, blended stepfamilies, non-traditional families. They have responsibilities for a generation older and one younger than they. With more complex families, there are more people to be considered. They may have to provide care for parents, grandparents, aunts, uncles, children, grandchildren, sisters and brothers. Each person in their extended family will have multiple and different needs. Somehow, they'll need to learn how to juggle their own needs as they age and the needs of those they call family.

Our systems for taking care of an aging population are being challenged at every turn. Budget crunches don't help. Staffing shortages don't help. Scant knowledge about gerontology doesn't help. There are many needs but fewer solutions.

I missed their generation by about 10 years and when these brash young things were coming into their own, I didn't appreciate them. Perhaps each of us likes to think that our generation is the one that's finally getting things right and we really don't want those nipping at our heels to make too many, if any, changes. Now, as I age, I think I can see that each generation builds on the one before, keeping what is good and improving what is not.

At least that's what I hope the Boomers are doing. They have the political clout to change the systems that need changing. Those of us older than them still have political power and savvy and know how to get things done. With new recruits we should be even more successful. Boomers will be talking to Boomers in government, health care, corporations and academia. They will have a common ground that should benefit us all.

There's lots written about the need for Boomers to prepare financially for retirement and although it's getting closer, I hope they are paying attention. There are fewer corporate and private pensions plans available now. Social Security appears to be an uncertainty. So I urge my slightly younger aging brothers and sisters to realize that you cannot reap unless you have planted.

I take back most of my shaking of head and frowning thoughts about your lifestyle when you were younger and welcome you to the new stage of seniority. I'm counting on your help. You are not alone.

nyc cop

June, 1981

I spent most of last weekend in the company of a police officer from New York City.

We met in the back of a church where he had come to act as best man at his brother's wedding where I was matron of honor for a very dear friend. Arriving late for the Friday evening rehearsal, Michael Campbell had a quick wit and ready smile that led to a series of jokes about how he had a "devil of a time" keeping to the speed limit. By the time we finished the rehearsal I knew this was no ordinary cop and asked if he'd consent to an interview about his job. It's probably the longest running question and answer exchange I've ever conducted. We were interrupted constantly by interested partygoers, who'd pick up on a word or two in passing, pausing to hear the discussion.

'Bodega Mike' as my new friend, Officer Campbell, was called in his area is the picture of a typical Irish policeman: ruddy complexion, sandy colored hair, witty and with a way with words that would charm the dew off a shamrock and instill confidence in a nervous citizen. His 'handle' of 'Bodega Mike' comes from the Spanish word for grocery store. Mike's beat included a number of Spanish grocers over whom he keeps a watchful eye. The use of a Spanish nickname would seem to indicate that this Irish cop has been accepted.

As a member of the Transit Police Department in New York City, Mike works in District 17 in the south Bronx. The area was recently featured in the Paul Newman movie, "Fort Apache, The Bronx." Mike's area is the Fort Apache that has been so named because of an attack launched on the district by the residents who lost one of their own. According to Mike, the movie accurately depicts much of what occurs regularly in their district.

Less accurate accounts of police life are found on television. "They don't get the whole story. They like to feature the sensational." His daily routine is not filled with one exciting case after another. In fact, he says there's a lot of boredom and repetition in his work. Why does he continue to go to work each day after 15 years on the force? "The challenge" he smiles. "There is something new every day and I hope I'll be able to handle whatever comes along."

The "ever present, inevitable gun" is part of the job and nothing more. He's had one close call when he was shot at by "a very professional person." In equally professional style, Mike called for his assailant to halt and when there was no response, Mike fired almost a full round. He did not hit the person attacking him who was able to get away in a fast green Cadillac. The next day Mike discovered he had "shot the heck out of a Gulf gas pump." He tells this story with obvious relief—he wasn't hurt, his assailant wasn't hurt. Mike was disappointed in losing the suspect but doesn't dwell on missed opportunities.

The gun incident brings into focus the danger police officers face every day. Mike's wife, Bea, says she tries not to think about it. "I think that he's going to work and that's all." She tries to keep things normal for their two children. When they hear of a shooting, they will all say they hope Dad is wearing his vest today.

"Lonely" and "scary" was Bea's response to how it feels to be a police officer's wife. She survives emotionally by "being my own person." Bea is a nurse and often does extra duty. She's mother and father for many of the children's activities. She considers him a good father and very helpful "when he's home."

Making friends is difficult for policemen. Often, people appear to think "we'll be a cop first and a friend second when push comes to shove. But that doesn't have to be the case."

Mike joined the force in 1966 because he wanted to try and help people. As for the worst part of his job, Mike dreads "telling a mother or father that their son is dead. This happens too often." What he really likes about his job is when he knows he's helped someone, whether it is a person who says, "I'm lost" or talking a potential suicide out of his intended action.

"As long as people are living and dying, we're on the scene."

what

"Bull-headed"

"Bullish on America"

"Like a bull in a china shop"

Our language is filled with cute references to these animals. We in Bundyville can now add our own appropriate phrase as we have our very own bull. There are undoubtedly many "b" words I could use to describe him but they really aren't fit to print.

The Bundyville Bull got loose last weekend and came to explore the world around him. He had four directions to go after breaking loose from his rope about a quarter of a mile south of us, but some whimsy brought him our way. Perhaps it was the smell of freshly painted furniture neatly lined up on our drive to dry in the bright sun and soft breezes that attracted him. As we were cleaning up our brushes, I looked up and saw a large black object heading down our neighbor's hill only a few hundred feet away heading right for us.

"Oh @#$%^%. Here comes a bull," I shrieked as I headed for the garage.

Bruce looked up. "A WHAT???" He queried in a very husbandly tone that indicated his wife had had too much sun and Harvest Gold paint.

"A BULL!" I repeated with great arm waving and pointing.

Sure enough. A young black bull from up the road was on the loose and exploring. Only I didn't want him to see any part of my world, thank you.

Calmly, Bruce strode over to the corner of the drive, placing himself between the approaching menace and the furniture (and, incidentally, me). He spoke gently to the animal and tried to cajole him into being a good boy. HA! Here was what Elmer was looking for—a playmate. He trotted around the furniture and up our drive, heading for the road. A few disbelieving drivers slowed down but when they got their chance, took off.

Meanwhile our great protector, Smokey, was visiting next door with Beth. He bravely barked at the intruder from afar but that was about all. Smokey was informing Elmer that he had crossed territorial limits but Elmer seemed oblivious. I tied Smokey up before he got a chance to prove whether any of his ancestral cattle-herding ability had sifted through to him. (One crisis at a time is enough for anyone, right?)

Of course, Beth wanted in on the action. It looked like fun listening to Dad trying to soft-talk Elmer, then berating him for going through the rose garden, then jogging along trying to corral him.

Old chicken, Mom, insisted that Beth stay out of the way and hustled her inside where we dashed from window to window watching the 'catch me if you can' routine outside. (Confidentially, from safe inside, it was pretty funny.)

Finally, my mind began to function on at least one cylinder. I found the telephone and called Elmer's owner who said she'd be right down. By then he'd found a nice safe place in the woods next to our neighbors and seemed content to stay.

Soon we could hear a dynamic little woman with a pail of grain in her arms giving her errant bull what-for and telling him in no uncertain terms to "git" and "git" he did with hardly a backward glance at his playmate nor the near havoc.

The following week I received a huge poster of a bull from a Merrill Lynch friend for the 'Best Bull Story'.

three cats: 27 lives? *May, 2005*

June is cat adoption month. We've been involved in three cat adoptions but with a twist: the cats adopted us.

Charlie was our first tabby who showed up at our doorstep, skinny, hungry and thirsty. We were delighted but chose to put some food and water on the porch for him just in case he was merely lost. We didn't want to become attached to someone else's pet. Soon it became apparent that Charlie had chosen our home to be his new one and we warmly welcomed him into the house.

We took him to a vet for a checkup, shots, and neutering and there was no doubt that he was ours. He took to inside living very well and only occasionally went back outdoors. When he did it was usually to bring me back a present in the form of a dead mouse, a bird, and even a fish almost his size. He would deposit these treasures on the front step so I'd be sure to be shocked when I found them.

My theory about his occasional hunting is that since he did this only when my husband was out of town, he was proving his manly protective abilities.

Basically I'm a chicken when it comes to critters, alive or dead, so our young daughter would grab a snow shovel and give the treasures a watery burial in the Oswego River, where she reasoned the food chain would take care of disposal.

Unfortunately for Charlie, during one of his excursions he was hit on the road and didn't survive. Although he'd been 'ours' for only a few years, all three of us were mightily upset.

A few years later, after we'd lost a beloved puppy to another road accident, Boots showed up. We repeated the food and water routine. One very rainy night with lightning and thunder, our daughter came in and knocked on my husband's sleeping head to wake him. She could hear a cat meowing outside and knew that they had to save it.

So, father and daughter in full rain gear with flashlights went out to save the cat. After a good drenching and about an hour's search, they were heading back into the house when the meowing became louder. They found her hiding behind the doghouse and brought her in. We wrapped warm towels around her until she stopped shaking then gave her a comfy spot to sleep and she was part of the family for the next 10 years, never going outside again.

We moved from our rural New York setting to Cleveland and then to Kentucky and Boots came as part of the family, sitting atop our clothing in the back of a station wagon looking quite regal. After three years in Kentucky, she became filled with cancer and we did the humane thing.

I vowed there would be no more cats in the house. We were going to be empty nesters, were considering retirement in a few years, no cat was going to tear up my heart again.

On my 50th birthday a true waif of a tabby kitten appeared. She was small, abused, scarred and not sure about people. We did the food and water outdoor thing for a week then one night when I was alone she hopped from the porch floor about six feet up to the kitchen window sill and gave me such a sad look that I opened the door and in she scooted. I decided an appropriate name would be "5-0" and for the next 14 years she was ours.

I have wondered over the years whether, since all three cats looked and acted very similar, was it one cat with three lives, or did we have three cats who had a collective 27 lives?

We had almost 30 years of wonderful tabby companions so I guess their adoption plan worked.

puppies *February, 1976*

For the past few months at our house we've been testing cartoonist Charles Schulz' theory that "Happiness is a warm puppy." The creator of the Peanuts characters must have had our daughter, Beth, in mind when he wrote that.

Smokey is the "warm puppy" that came into our lives just after Christmas when he was three months old. His mother is a purebred collie and his father is mostly a German shepherd. Shortly after the large litter was born we made the mistake of leaving Beth with the owner for a day when she became well acquainted with the balls of fluff. Even several weeks later when we had finally given in to the idea of getting a puppy, Beth remembered the one she had fallen in love with.

And it's been a continuing love story. Girl and dog have been inseparable outdoors. Wherever you see the red snowsuit you see a wagging tail close behind. When she slid down the hill on her toboggan he was either sitting behind her or chasing after. When she slid down in her nylon snowsuit he put his front paws on her shoulders and his hind feet went a mile a minute to keep up.

Before we brought Smokey home, we bought a dog care book to adequately prepare ourselves. As I glanced over it I noticed many similarities between it and my baby care book.

"The normal care and training of dogs involve no great mysteries. The application of common sense and good judgment is required, however." Shades of Dr. Spock!!!

"Puppies left alone will bark, moan and whine. If, in pity, you go to the howling puppy, he will howl every time you leave him. Suffer one night, two nights or possibly three and you'll have it made." Now where had I read that before?

Even the suggestions for feeding and discipline smack of a good child routine. But I have discovered one thing: Pampers are a lot easier to clean up after.

Moving a new animal into the neighborhood unannounced had its effect on the big black cat next door. Frisky has been used to the run of both properties and was less than pleased when this bouncing new "thing" appeared on what he considered his turf. Smokey was used to cats and thought Frisky was a new playmate. Not so! As Frisky recoiled, stretched every hair on his body to double length, sizzled at Smokey and bared his claws, we realized that friendship between neighbors does not necessarily transfer to their animals.

Despite all my protests that he was not MY dog, when no one's looking, I do soften up considerably. The first day after the Christmas break when the house was empty I vowed I wasn't going to be one of those pet owners who carries on a conversation with said pet. Well, that lasted about a day. The next morning I allowed him into the space I call my office. I've written columns under some challenging situations but Smokey adds a whole new dimension. He wedges his body between my feet, the typewriter table and the desk. Yes, there is enough of him to fill all the gaps. He doesn't care for the sound of my electric typewriter or perhaps he's making editorial comments. He curls up in the kneehole section of the desk but soon gets bored and starts to chase his tail—quite a feat in a small space for an ever-growing animal.

We had to purchase larger food and water bowls and chose the no-tip, no-spill, bite and crack resistant type. All these provided a challenge. The first evening after dinner, he carried the bowl as far as his rope would allow and flung it several more feet. He's certainly challenging the truth-in-advertising rules.

My neighbors are seeing some strange sights these days—several times, early in the morning but always after husband and daughter are gone, Smokey manages to entangle himself around a tree, a pole, anything he can in ways that would defeat even Houdini. I pull on boots and warm coat and trudge out with my nightie and robe flapping in the cold winter wind, muttering as I go. His joy at seeing me usually brings a small smile but I don't give in easily. We've tried to tangle-proof his play area but I have the sinking feeling that he's smarter than we are. One of the best things he does is bark at the oil deliveryman. At today's prices, Smokey is giving voice to my sentiments.

Yes, Mr. Schulz, "Happiness is a warm puppy."

A few months later, Smokey broke away from his rope and ran across the road. He was hit by a car and killed instantly. It was a very sad time.

casts *October, 1974*

We've just completed a rather unusual five weeks at our house. On Labor Day, our four-year old daughter had an unfortunate tangle with a bicycle, which left her with a fractured right leg necessitating a cast from hip to toes.

It's been quite an experience for us three. Beth is a very active youngster, on the go from morning 'til night, up and down trees, off and on her tricycle, back and forth on a swing, zooming down the slide, almost constantly in motion. To be told to keep her quiet for the first few days, to keep the injured leg up as much as possible seemed like an impossible situation for me. Then it dawned on me; this was only for the first days followed by weeks of no walking, running, climbing or riding.

As so often happens with children, I was pleasantly surprised. Once she realized she could move her leg and the pain experienced before the cast was gone, she began moving around rather well on her own with a crawl more awkward than when she was an infant but it still got her where she wanted to go. The rented child-size wheelchair gave her another dimension of mobility and independence. She could maneuver around part of the house and was able to attend preschool, thanks to a kind teacher.

I had a few adaptions to make myself. I had forgotten how much self-care she did for herself but now needed help in all stages of dressing, bathing, getting into bed, moving from one floor to another. She also needed close supervision to keep her weight off the right leg. One afternoon I took her outside for some fresh air, dashed back inside for a moment, returned to see her coming down the small slide, right leg high in the air, the rest of her moving at top speed. What a sight! What a fright!

While there were some rough times, we had some precious moments. We spent a lazy sunny afternoon watching the sun shimmering across the river making millions of golden coins on the rippling water. Another afternoon was spent watching a family of little yellow birds in our big pine tree. Her squeals of delight didn't scare them off and I wondered if perhaps they were entertaining their immobile friend. We spent time watching chipmunks and squirrels hoarding acorns for the winter months. She noticed each change of color of the leaves on the riverbank.

The first cold, wet autumn morning we lit a fire and spent the day cuddled close to its warmth and worked on a jigsaw puzzle. In between puzzle pieces there were some serious questions: Where does God go on rainy days? Does He have a fire with His mom?

We tried to maintain as normal a routine as possible, even to her continuing to 'help' Dad cut the lawn as she rode sidesaddle on his lap and Mom almost fainted. We learned that sometimes it's no fun to watch a friend chase a bunny rabbit across the field and not be running too. It's no thrill to cheer the neighbors' soccer game when you can't be part of the action. It's hard to sit at the kitchen window and watch the dog next door run back and forth and not be out there playing with him.

Beth made the five weeks as easy as she could and I found myself filled with pride as I watched her cope with the first real problem of her life.

overdue apology *September, 1999*

I owe my daughter a major apology.

When she was four years old she spent almost six weeks in a cast to heal a broken leg. The cast went from her toes to her hip and was an inconvenience for a very active young person. When the cast was removed, she wouldn't walk using that leg because she told us, "My mind tells me I can't walk."

What can you possibly say to someone who really believed she couldn't walk without assistance? I truly can't remember what I said to her but I do recall alternating between pity and anger. She could ride her tricycle at high speeds; she could somehow scoot up to the top of the slide on the jungle gym set and come barreling down. She couldn't walk.

We found a solution in an unlikely source: ski boots. She was hoping to learn to ski that winter so Dad put the ski boots on her and said she'd have to walk well before she could consider getting on skis. For several evenings after dinner there was a ski boot exercise around the kitchen and before long she realized she really could walk on her own.

Twenty-six years later I broke my left arm close to the shoulder thus had a cast from my shoulder to my fingers. My LEFT arm, without which I am helpless, and so it remained for six weeks.

A few days before my arm cast was removed, she told me not to expect too much of a miraculous change. She added that now I would more fully understand why she couldn't walk after her cast came off.

She was absolutely right! And I have officially told her that I am sorry for not understanding the difficulty she was having. Even with my arm I had trouble comprehending why it wasn't 100 percent after the bulky cast was no longer there. And I'm a lot older than four so should have known healing would take time, a lot more time than if I'd been four.

While giving me advance warning about how my arm might feel post-cast, she left out lots of specifics. She didn't tell me that my "good" left hand still wouldn't be able to reach my mouth for either feeding or application of lipstick. Brushing my teeth is still done with my "wrong" right hand and flossing isn't even considered. She didn't tell me that simple things like putting on a string of pearls and matching earrings would still need help from another pair of hands.

There are several items of a personal nature that women wear which need two good hands. Once again we experienced the problems of a right-handed engineer and a left-handed klutz trying to work together while neither of us had a fully functioning left arm. Lots of silly situations made us laugh and that's what got us through.

At least when Beth was in a cast she was easy to dress and could feed herself and let's face it, clothing for a four-year-old is simpler than for someone who started this ordeal as a 60-year-old and became 61 along the way.

I may be starting a dangerous precedent with a full-fledged apology. I undoubtedly have many more things that I may have to admit that she was right about and I was not. Hard as it may be to acknowledge mistakes, large or small, this is one error that time has brought full circle. However, no ski boots or golf clubs are going to be used to bribe me into getting back full use of this arm. I'm going with Dr. Oakley's prediction about God and Mother Nature taking care.

lefty

August, 2012

It's not easy being left-handed in a right-handed world.

I have complained and whined about this for most of my life.

A simple task, like using a manual can opener, can become a frustrating chore. The can opener is designed to be used by right-handed people. So we who are left-handed have to adapt to survive. So what's the big deal, you may wonder. It's not natural for us to take a tool designed for the majority of the world and use it backwards. Eventually some of us give in and do it the other way, gritting our teeth and muttering at the same time.

Scissors are perhaps the greatest challenge. For them to cut what you want, sharp side has to meet sharp side. I have gone through many gyrations trying to cut open a package, some fabric, or an article from the paper. Upside down and backwards isn't fun nor is it pretty. I learned to cope. Then my mother-in-law who, like her son, had spasms watching me cut something, bought me a pair of left-handed scissors. What a thoughtful gift! When I went to use them I discovered I had adapted so well to the wrong-sided ones that I now had to unlearn one series of skills and learn a new set. Finally I found a pair of kitchen scissors that have equally shaped sides and can be used successfully by either hand. A triumph for some left-handed inventor.

Such trivial things as loading the dishwasher are different for me—if I open the machine and all the plates are facing right to left, I realize my right-handed daughter has loaded the machine. My right-handed husband, on the other hand (no pun intended) follows my style of left-to-right. I believe that is what is called a learned behavior.

The layout of our kitchen cupboards has my stamp all over—my family has lived with this reverse pattern so long that they don't even question it anymore.

We had a lovely gentleman painting the interior of our house. He was so meticulous, even removing items from closets to paint the interior. When I went to put my clothes back they were in reverse order. That showed me, yet one more time, that I'm the odd one. He was a right-handed painter, had been for years, and did a wonderful job.

Not only is my husband right-handed, but he's also an engineer. (Enough said for those of you married to engineers.) A left-handed klutz living with a right-handed engineer is not necessarily a perfect situation.

My mother was left-handed and on my first day at school she told the teacher NOT to make me change. Her mother had done the same—quite forward thinking for women in the 20s and 50s. Because of their efforts I feel I must keep up my southpaw, lefty tendencies.

Consider that until a few hundred years ago being left-handed indicated you were an evil person and all sort of devil myths were built up around us. At least today the worst someone can say about us is how awkward our writing looks.

And, best of all, I'm in great company: Julia Roberts is left-handed and so is Prince William!

dogs *February, 1975*

I've finally gone to the dogs!

But I wasn't alone.

On a recent Wednesday evening (in West Palm Beach) 4,120 of us went to the dogs and spent $248,148 while we were at it. That averages out to a little over $60 a person. Someone else must have spent a lot more to make up the difference for what I didn't spend.

I was at one of Florida's several kennel clubs where greyhound racing is a nightly activity for thousands—from little old ladies in tennis shoes to little old ladies drenched in diamonds and driving Caddies, parked in the valet section, of course.

I was lucky. No, I didn't win, but since we didn't arrive until the ninth race of a twelve race card, I had only one-fourth the chance to bet, thus to lose. And then I wasn't so lucky. The man selling programs had deserted his post. Now I know why, "You can't tell a thing without a program" is such an important phrase. Programs are supposed to guide you in your careful selection of a sure thing on which to bet. Supplementing that is the list from the morning paper, carefully clipped out and placed on the kitchen counter, still waiting for you when you come home.

Greyhound racing is quite different from horse racing. You get to lose your money in about thirty seconds instead of two minutes. The dogs chase "Rusty" around the track and never catch him, or her, or it. The half-mile track has a beautiful reflecting pool in the infield and is surrounded by elegant royal palms swaying in the breeze. So there are some consolations.

How did I do? Not well. Without a program I had to rely on feminine intuition (which is grossly overrated, girls). In my first race there was a dog named "Annie's Pride" so, of course, I had to choose her. She tried hard but only came in third and I'd planned on a win or place position for her. So much for the meaningful names theory.

Next race I chose the two black dogs because they were the only two of their kind in the race. One of them was named Swinger, so how could I lose? Swinger must have swung too hard the night before and decided to take it easy for this race. So much for the name and physical characteristics theory.

In the eleventh race, I bet my age for the quinella and chose the lower number for an across-the-board bet. The higher number came in and was such a long shot the payouts were great. I'd chosen the wrong half of my age number so I wasn't in the small select group of winners. So much for the age theory.

Finally I thought I had a real winner in the last race with Wego Sue sounding so close to Oswego that I was convinced. No doubt the thought of snow and cold kept her distracted and she didn't come in. So much for the hometown theory.

All in all it was a fun evening but I think I'll stick to horses or perhaps the Florida phenomenon of Jai-Lai where it can take up to ten minutes to lose your bet. At least I'd get some screaming and yelling for my money.

Friendship *August, 2000*

There's something very special about old friends—those people who have known you for a long time and like you anyway.

This week some old friends relocated to the Sandhills from Connecticut and we are delighted to have them back in the same area code. We've known each other for more than 30 years. Our daughters are the same age. We've been through some great times together and have seen each other through some not so great times.

Although we moved around before settling here, we were always just a phone call away. And although we love e-mail, it doesn't replace the sound of a friend's voice. A close friend's voice sometimes tells you much more than the words being spoken. After many years of keeping in touch, it doesn't take a lot of deductive reasoning to know when something is wrong, or your friend is sad, or she is happy, or worried, or just glad to share some feelings with you. Often, just talking makes life brighter for both.

Old friends knew you before you filled your resume with impressive entries, or rose to the top in your field, and they still like you. They share your success and are ready to console during failure. They know your political views, and like you anyway. They accept you for who you are because they've been along for the ride as you grew to be that person, and like you anyway.

Old friends are usually happy to just be with you.

They don't need an agenda. You can sit and visit into the wee hours of the night or you can silently enjoy a magnificent view. You can shop 'til you drop or prop your feet up and spend hours just enjoying the fact of friendship with no rules, no demands, no expectations.

We have been very lucky in having good friends in all the places we've lived. Over the years we've lost touch with some but those who were, are, and will be friends for life are among our blessings to be counted. Friends from different places are like an onion—there is the core of folks who've known us forever, and each place we've lived, another layer or two has been added. Each layer has its own characteristic and when added with others, gives us an amazing cross-section of people.

Old friends remember your birthdays and anniversaries. They know which foods you enjoy. They know the kind of music you like and the movies you'd go to see, or not. They remember the names of your family members as if they were their own. They are interested in what's going on in the lives of those who matter to you.

As we age, old friends are even more special. We have a shared history that makes us feel "at home" in each other's company. We don't have to explain to them where we've been and what we've done. They know what illnesses we've had, probably what medications we take, and could easily speak for us in an emergency if need be.

Since moving to the Sandhills three years ago, we've made many new friends whom we hope will become old friends. Retirement is a new stage of life and being able to share with others enjoying this stage helps form a bond. Today's golfing buddy or bridge partner may easily be tomorrow's soul mate.

We are looking forward to sharing our old friends with our more recent ones. We know that they, too, will make new friends here and we look forward to meeting them.

Nesting *January, 2002*

Some call it "nesting." Others think it's "hibernating." I think it's wonderful.

I'm referring to a perceived "new" lifestyle trend, which implies that we are spending more time in our homes with our families. We seem to be forsaking high living and extremes in style, both in home decorating and clothing, for comfort.

During this past holiday season, USA Today reported that more of us stayed at home on New Year's Eve or spent the evening with friends at their homes. We also stayed home more during the season from Thanksgiving Day through New Year's Day. (It doesn't take a rocket scientist to understand that since September 11th we want to feel safe and comfortable. We don't want to be in crowded places.)

Whoever the style setters are, it doesn't take them long to see a shift in our lifestyles and to quickly put a name on it to help market new things for a very old idea.

The nesting idea appeals to me. It always has. I like to be comfortable in my surroundings. I like to use whatever is at hand to make our home comfortable, and those who visit. When I visit an absolutely spectacularly decorated home, I am impressed. But I'm not usually comfortable. If I sat down on the sofa with its perfectly matched pillows coordinated with the plush carpet, I worry that I might move something, even slightly, that would ruin the whole picture.

Casual is more to my liking. I want people to come in, sit down and enjoy. If they move a few things, that's fine with me. In reality, my husband and I are the ones who live in our home all the time. If it pleases us, then that's good enough. We've always liked to make sure there's room for others but at this stage in our lives, a couple of big comfy recliners with a good view of the great outdoors are pretty close to perfect. Since we share our living space with a 12-year-old cat—really it is she who shares her living space with us—we are careful about choice of fabric. She seems to prefer things with a little texture so the "good" chairs she likes have towels covering the seat area. (We do try to remove these when "company" is coming.)

My one concession to a little more formal style is our dining room, which has a number of antique family pieces and they deserve proper display and use.

The nesting idea conjures up pictures of birds dashing to and fro to make a nest for their new family. They are very precise about location and material and look quite comfortable and settled when they're done. Ospreys are so particular about their location that once they have found the ideal spot, they come back year after year and just build on top of last year's model.

Because we moved a number of times in our pre-retirement life, I think that's why one home, one place appeals to me so much. When we come back after being away for even a day or so, there's a joint "aaaah" as we open the door and know we are back home.

During our recent snow event, I thought being forced to stay indoors was just great. Most of the people with whom I had telephone conversations were baking bread or making soups or stews. We did the bread and stew thing. The house smelled wonderful, we were snug and well fed. A little down time the week after New Year's is a great way to prepare for whatever's coming our way.

n-o-t-h-i-n-g *October, 1999*

"I just can't imagine doing *nothing* all day, every day," proclaimed a family friend.

"Nothing?" I said, getting ready for a full court press to respond. "Look at my calendar and see what *nothing* looks like."

She was quite brave in repeating her feelings in a group where only one other person was still employed outside the home and getting a paycheck. Her husband is one of us in the doing *nothing* crowd, unless you count volunteer coaching, organizing various events, and playing championship bridge. I quickly realized that his activities seem like *nothing* to her but are very needed and appreciated in his community.

Those of us who have chosen this *nothing* existence have done it after years of a daily grind and now we are reaping the rewards of that other life. Few of us believed we would be doing *nothing* and, in fact, few of us are.

RSVP offers almost 50 agencies with a wide assortment of needs. In truth, who but retired people have the time to commit to daily meal delivery or weekly tutoring? SCORE has ready, willing and able former businessmen to lend a hand to small businesses. Almost every church and school in the county needs help on a regular basis. The Moore County Office of the Aging has many more needs than it has people to fulfill these needs. The new Senior Resource Center will offer programs and provide resources for anyone wishing to remain active and not sit around doing *nothing.*

Social activities are another important aspect of life. Golf and bridge are two of the more popular ones here in the Sandhills, but they are not the only activities. Keeping active, mentally and physically, can contribute to our well being. Many studies have proven that people who are happy are healthier. So not even a regular game of bridge can be considered *nothing* when it helps us stay connected with others.

Those contemplating retirement should follow a few of our Sandhills retirees around for a week, or even a day, to learn what this *nothing* life has to offer.

When we retired, I posted a large calendar in the kitchen and have slowly retrained my husband to write everything down. (I'm not the one who needs to keep track of tee times.) The calendar is to be consulted before agreeing to do anything. Our first Christmas here, we had to check the calendar to make a date to go Christmas shopping.

Several friends have said they wonder how they ever had time to work. At first, I thought that was an exaggeration. If anything, it's an understatement. Working for pay consumed many of us for most of our lives. Now, working for fun, doing what we want is the order of the day. We can choose where we will labor and enjoy that work because it often involves making life better for someone else and allowing us to indulge in self-satisfaction.

I was surprised at my reaction to this *nothing* comment. I guess I resented having my life reduced to zero simply because I was now happily living among the retired. I thought I was living a life filled with challenges and satisfactions and some fun. Of course, the perfect response always comes long after the event. Next time, my response will be to smile widely and say, "Yes, and it's wonderful!"

cultural literacy *January, 2002*

About 10 years ago a wonderful book, *Cultural Literacy,* by E. D. Hirsch, Jr. sought to explain that background information about life was important to fully understanding the written or spoken word. Hirsch points out that to be fully literate people need to be familiar with a set of common, frequently used terms and phrases. He includes 5,000 names, dates, phrases and concepts.

A year or so later *The Dictionary of Cultural Literacy* appeared to explain many of the concepts from the first book, thus proving his point: we don't know all that we should about our cultural history.

It appears that at least one institution of higher learning, Beloit College in Wisconsin, has taken the cultural literacy message to heart. Thanks to Charles Kerr in Pinehurst, I received a list which the Beloit staff puts together each year to try to give the faculty a sense of the mind-set of incoming freshmen. The people who will start college this year were born in 1982.

> They have no meaningful recollection of the Reagan Era and probably did not know that he had ever been shot.
>
> They were prepubescent when the Persian Gulf War was waged.
>
> Black Monday 1987 is as significant to them as the Great Depression.
>
> There has only been one Pope.
>
> They were 11 when the Soviet Union broke apart and do not remember the Cold War.

They have never feared a nuclear war.

They are too young to remember the space shuttle blowing up.

Tiananmen Square means nothing to them.

Their lifetime has always included AIDS.

Bottle caps have always been screw-off and plastic.

Atari predates them, as do vinyl albums. The expression 'you sound like a broken record' means nothing to them. They have never owned a record player. They may never have heard of an eight-track tape. The compact disk was introduced when they were one year old.

As far as they know, stamps have always cost about 33 cents.

Most have never seen a TV with only 13 channels nor have they seen a black and white set. They have always had cable and probably remote controls. There have always been VCRs but they have no idea what Beta is.

They were born the year Sony introduced Walkman.

Roller-skating has always meant 'inline' for them.

Jay Leno has always been the host of The Tonight Show.

They have never seen Larry Bird play.

The Vietnam War is as ancient to them as WWI and WWII and the Civil War.

They have no idea that Americans were ever held hostage in Iran.

They can't imagine what hard contact lenses are.

They've never heard: 'I'd walk a mile for a Camel'; 'Where's the beef'; or 'de plane, de plane.'

They do not care who shot J.R. because they have no idea who J.R. is.

Kansas, Chicago, Boston, America and Alabama are places not groups.

There has always been MTV.

They don't have a clue how to use a typewriter.

"Do you feel old yet," Charlie asked.

"No. Just very culturally illiterate."

basketball *March, 2001*

Aaaaaah!

That giant sigh you heard this past Tuesday morning came from those who are not dyed in the (blue) wool basketball fans. March Madness is over and we have a champion.

To really appreciate the game I think you have to be born into the culture of an avid basketball following. I was not, even though a Canadian, Dr. Naismith, is credited with inventing the game.

I went to an all-girl convent high school. We did not have an athletic program. If we had brothers or boyfriends who went to co-ed public schools, we may have developed an interest in their sports.

My first real exposure to the college game came when we lived about a half hour north of Syracuse. If you weren't an Orange fan you had a lonesome time during both football and basketball seasons. I can remember when Jim Boeheim was named the Orange basketball coach. He's lost a little hair but looks like the same man we first got to know as he built (or did he rebuild?) the Syracuse team.

I started reading sports pages back then in order to have some understanding of what people were talking about at parties, on the street, at the beauty salon, or in the grocery store. As a reporter trying to fit in with the mostly male press corps covering various levels of government in our area, I liked to have at least a passing knowledge of the really big sports stories. Such information has come in handy during my 20-year Trivial Pursuit marathon with my brother, and more recently for the occasional question on "Who Wants to be a Millionaire?"

My conversion to basketball continued when we moved to Kentucky. I thought Syracuse fans were dedicated! Ha! Kentucky had them beat by a country mile. If you weren't a Wildcats or Cardinals fan, you didn't count for much. Being a Wildcat was considered preferable to a Cardinal. When I became involved at Western Kentucky University, it was important to support the Hilltoppers, particularly the Lady Hilltoppers who consistently had good teams.

Just when I was getting into this whole March Madness thing, we moved to Michigan where we had either the Wolverines or Spartans to cheer for. I had to learn new names and recognize new team colors. As I am not an avowed fan, I usually went for whoever seemed most likely to come out as winners. To the *real* fan, I no doubt sound shallow. So be it. If you don't have a lifelong affection for one team, then it seems to make sense to go with whoever's on top.

Coming to North Carolina has greatly enhanced my basketball education. People here breathe and eat basketball. Shortly after we arrived, Dean Smith retired—I had never seen such intense press coverage of a college coach. I fully expected to read that he could walk on water. (To those of you who think he can, I apologize. I just haven't seen that side of him, or coaching, or the game.)

This year I actually watched whole games, not my usual final five minutes when I happen to believe that's when the important stuff happens. I didn't wait until the Final Four; I began with the games leading up to the field of 64, then the first round, and succeeding rounds until it got down to two. With my past history, I had Syracuse,

Kentucky, Michigan State and a couple of teams from our state to watch. Some fell by the wayside early so I moved on to the next tier.

It was an interesting exercise, but I won't miss not hearing about the madness and the pressures of getting to be national champion.

North Carolina has converted me; I am now a better fan. In 2015 I came out on top of a basketball pool, what's not to like?

Computers *February, 2002*

A few weeks ago our computer was infected with a virus and had to go to the computer hospital to be cured.

As the one in the family who now uses the computer a great deal, I was totally lost without it. The great irony is that both my husband and daughter brought me, kicking and screaming, into the computer age. "You'll love it, Mom!" "It'll make writing a lot easier, dear." "You won't believe how you ever did without it."

Those were some of their arguments. Naturally the unspoken major incentive—for them—was that they wanted a computer. They wanted one immediately. They wanted to do spreadsheets and play games. If they could work me into the schedule, then perhaps I could manage the word processing.

Both during last January's storm, and this year's "hospitalization of the computer" I had to admit they were right. I haven't quite said I was wrong, but did admit to reluctance.

We bought our first computer, the dinosaur Commodore 64, in 1982. It served us well with games, and word processing. When I began to explore the wonders of Print Shop, I did secretly admit that maybe I had been a little slow to embrace the computer world. We have moved up the food chain a few times, getting newer and better "stuff." I am bothered by having to learn a new technique to make something turn out the way I want, and it seems that once I've mastered the change, it's time to upgrade again.

As a person who started in the newspaper business in the days of hot lead type hammered out by a linotype operator, I am constantly amazed at the ease with which we can now type an article for the paper, make changes to it even after we're finished, and transmit material electronically from site to site. Emblazoned in my mind is the image of Hans, an imposing composing room supervisor to whom you'd have to sell your soul to get even a slight change in a story or a headline, never mind changing a picture. He and his crew worked by a strict set of rules: we wrote the content but they put it together; we mapped out the pages but they put them together. In short, whatever Hans and his crew put together, no mere fledgling reporter or her boss or his boss was going to take apart.

Now, as I go about the business of writing a column or a feature or a news story, I move type around with abandon and I feel Hans turning over in his grave. The ability to correct spelling and grammar on the spot because squiggly green or red lines show up on the screen still amazes me. I accept the spelling suggestions but rail against the grammar "suggestions!" I reason that I've been using the English language longer than my computer and if I'm not doing it right by now, then I shouldn't be doing it. OK, now and then one of the grammar hints does make sense and I might give it a try.

I have an extra safety net at The Pilot—someone else reads my stuff before you see it. Clark Cox is usually copy editor for me and we seem to be in agreement most of the time. And if we weren't, Clark would win.

I really, really enjoy e-mail, and games, and sending electronic cards. My husband and daughter smile smugly as they see me working or playing on a machine that I was so reluctant to welcome into our lives. They were right again and I'm glad.

Written in the Heart *April, 2000*

"Where is it written," asks poet Judith Viorst, "that fathers get to have business trips to Brazil and mothers get to take the nursery school class to the fire station?"

As it happened when I first read this poem, my husband was on a business trip to Brazil and I was doing the nursery school thing.

"Where is it written?" became my catch phrase for a few years. I would wonder out loud where it was written that mothers had to do a long laundry list of things. Then one day my daughter stopped me in my tracks when I muttered one of my questions by answering: "On page 264 of the Mothers' Manual."

Few, if any of us, have a Mothers' Manual. But since a frequent response to her questions about doing something was often "No" and to the immediate response of "Why not?" I would say "Because it says so in the book," it was a reasonable assumption that I did refer to a book of some sort. That bluff lasted only a few years then she began to think logically and called my bluff about the oft-quoted nonexistent book. Now we joke about it and I still say, "Where is it written?"

A Mothers' Manual would have been a great thing to have on hand. I mean a *real* manual written by *real* mothers, people who had been through whatever crisis I was in. I did not live close to my own mother when I was a new mother.

Today there are many helpful books out there starting with what to expect during pregnancy on through to the teenage years and probably beyond. When I was a mother, I had Dr. Spock and was grateful. I also had some good friends. If you're lucky enough to find a close friend with similar values and ideas about childrearing, a manual isn't quite as necessary. Still, even the best of friends doesn't want to hear from you in the middle of the night when she's trying to catch some much needed sleep herself.

Beth can mark the first years of her life with scars: split chin at age one while finding out what stairs were all about; cut on the side of her eye that needed stitches—she'd been jumping on a bed; stitches in the center of her forehead at age three from falling against the corner of a wall as her buddy tried to pick her up; broken leg at age four from riding on the back of an older child's bicycle. The Emergency Room personnel knew us by name. No manual could have prepared me for any of these incidents and I doubt that any reassurance could have made me feel better.

There's no manual for comforting your child after a major disappointment, no matter how insignificant it may appear to us. Not getting the teacher of choice, or playing on the team you want, or sitting next to your best friend are disappointments that need soothing and explaining. And, you think, would that these were the only disappointments in life.

Now there are books about death and dying but when your child's only grandfather dies you can't just refer her to a book. Another significant death was that of a much-loved dog. That prompted her to announce that God doesn't always answer your prayers.

I guess each mother writes her own manual and you're not likely to find it on a bookshelf. We carry them around in our minds and hearts and hope that each choice will, at best, be helpful, and, at worst, do no harm.

Eloquent words and stirring music have permeated our lives in the weeks since September 11. Daily press briefings have brought forth some of most gut-wrenching feelings of those in high places and those not so high.

When we say, "we'll never be the same again," we're right. I'm hoping for a better society for all of us now that our attention has been tuned to the important things in life. Suddenly the nagging complaints of early September look miniscule in comparison with really tragic events.

Personally, I have found great comfort in music. Even the oft' repeated "Amazing Grace," "God Bless America," "The Battle Hymn of the Republic" and the haunting "Taps" have provided comfort. A bittersweet comfort, but comfort nonetheless.

In the car on September 11 and 12 when it seemed as if the radio news could get no worse, and yet it did, we periodically turned it off and played some favorite CDs for relief. Our choices were all Irish—when we left home on September 5 we did not anticipate the need for American music. Many of the songs have a certain pathos to them. "Danny Boy" is a prime example. We ran the gamut of sad songs to pub songs and then turned back to the radio for news. We repeated this pattern often and it helped a lot.

Once home, we loaded many patriotic songs and they've been playing much more frequently than usual. Aaron Copland's "Fanfare for the Common Man" is a perfect tribute for those still working at Ground Zero. His "Appalachian Spring" offers hope to the victims' families. John Williams with the Boston Pops plays all the rousing songs we usually hear around July 4th—"America," "This Land is Your Land," "America the Beautiful," and "New York, New York" are soothing to work to, or to just enjoy.

An Irving Berlin collection is a must. If we ever need reminding of the importance of immigrants to this country, listen to his "God Bless America"—and if you're really lucky, you'll hear Kate Smith singing.

A series of selections on a grand piano on a "Celebrate Freedom" disc makes me turn up the volume to levels that I used to chastise my daughter for. This collection covers everything from the national anthem to "Let There Be Peace on Earth" and I find it refreshes me each time it plays.

Then some old favorites celebrating different regions of the country draw my attention to the whole country—"Shenandoah," "My Old Kentucky Home," "The Streets of Laredo," "The Yellow Rose of Texas," "Nantucket Sunrise," "The Banks of the Ohio," "The Wabash," "Carry Me Back to Old Virginny," remind us of the wonderful variety we have in our many states.

The last CD to play is titled "Serenity" with Phil Coulter playing such peaceful songs as "Morning Has Broken," "The Bells of Angelus," "Bless This House," "The Lord is My Shepherd," and "Ave Maria."

It is proving true that music soothes the savage beast. Music is a sign of a civilized society. It is an important part of history showing that our society encouraged many forms of music. Sometimes when words fail us, a simple song will bridge the gap and get us on to the next step. When the Broadway community came together for the "New York, New York" commercial they reassured us that life would go on, including wonderful words and music.

alzheimer's *September, 2001*

My first close encounter with an Alzheimer's victim happened on Christmas Eve, 1988. My mother had a mild stroke during a family dinner and was taken to the emergency room of a major metropolitan hospital.

It was a dark, snowy night with almost impassable roads and we were about 10 miles from the hospital. After making the call to 911 we wondered if the ambulance would be able to get to us, as side roads had not been plowed. We dispatched the younger set to watch for the ambulance and direct it to us. Remarkably very little time elapsed and while we waited my mother began to come around.

She eventually felt she didn't need the hospital but the EMS technicians, recognizing that the weather was deteriorating and the need for additional care, cajoled her into going with them. My brother went in the ambulance with her. We followed, dropping off three aunts who had been with us for dinner and family time.

When I got to the hospital waiting room I asked for information and, getting none, went back to where my mother was sitting up, quite perky. As I stood there and watched for help to come our way, a lady in a bed across from her sat right up and started to scream at me. At first she startled me. I thought she was one of the drunks that were starting to arrive at the emergency room. I asked a nurse what was going on and was told she was an Alzheimer's patient.

Suddenly my mother's problems didn't seem so serious. She was now alert and eager to converse with the doctor, nurse, me, anyone who would talk to her. By the time she was observed and released, around 2 in the morning, my mother was in better shape than the rest of us!

But the other woman was not. She was in one of a long line of beds, partially hidden by a curtain, her lights dimmed. She went from utter silence to screaming with no apparent trigger. There was no one by her side, holding her hand or offering comfort.

She was totally alone for the four or five hours we were there. It just didn't seem right to have that happen on Christmas Eve when families all over the city were either already together or planning to be together.

I remember having negative thoughts about her family. Now that I know more about Alzheimer's disease, I understand why perhaps no one was with her. There may have been no one. If there were, then perhaps they were trying to have some semblance of a normal family holiday together, knowing that their loved one was safe in the hands of the hospital staff.

It couldn't have been an easy decision for that woman's family but it was a necessary one. They could do nothing to alleviate her symptoms. She was not in pain. I have no idea how she got to the hospital, but any number of possibilities comes to mind.

That was 12 years ago. We didn't know then what we know now. Since hers was the first human face I'd seen with Alzheimer's it has stayed with me. If I, a complete stranger, wanted to help but didn't know what to do, how hard must it have been for others in her life.

My mother continued to have small strokes with each one diminishing her capacity somewhat. Eventually she was said to have "dementia" which isn't pleasant but is still a far cry from an Alzheimer's diagnosis.

Random Acts of Kindness

January, 2008

You know that an idea has caught on when there are books and sequels written about it. "Random Acts of Kindness" is one such idea.

At one time we have all performed a "random" kindness for someone or had something kind done for us. For many, it's a way of life. They don't set out a plan of kindness but they just do kind things day in and day out.

I have mixed feeling about the formal writing down of this perfectly natural human act. On the one hand, it is interesting to read of many creatively kind things people do for each other. Perhaps some inspiration can be taken.

On the other hand, "random" loses some of its meaning now that we have somewhat formalized the phrase. Yet, better to keep the idea alive and introduce it to those who may not have made this a part of their lives.

One of the nicest things that came to my husband, completely as a surprise, was being handed a ticket to the final day of the U.S. Open. A lady was leaving the grounds and passed by him as he stood on the other side of the fence. Her daughter had gotten ill and she had to leave; she offered him her ticket.

This act proved to me the "casting bread upon the water" theory. About 10 years ago, he had been hosting a group of businessmen on a dinner cruise aboard the General Jackson in Opryland, just outside Nashville. Two guests didn't show. The ticket office refused to change the tickets or give him credit. He took the tickets and handed them to a young couple in a line waiting for possible cancellations. He made their day. The lady in Pinehurst made his.

Something I've done for years when traveling is to offer to take pictures of a family or group in front of a famous site. It's hard to get everyone in a picture unless an outsider does this. My most interesting encounter was on a cold, blustery day at Niagara Falls where a small group of Japanese visitors were trying to take group shots with each other's cameras. I speak no Japanese. They spoke no English. Yet in the universal language of smiling, and bowing, and pointing, we were able to get a group shot using each person's camera. I had truly never thought of that as a random act of kindness until a close friend pointed out the number of times I've done that on the spur of the moment. I feel that some of those people now make the offer to others.

Every time you pause in traffic to let someone make a difficult left turn, you are doing a random act of kindness. Each time you refrain from letting a driver who has done something really stupid know how you feel, you're being kind.

When you're playing your favorite sport (mine happens to be bridge), kindness comes into play when you don't say something about the way the play has gone. If it's not necessary to life or limb, why make an issue. On the other hand, a hearty "well done" goes a long way to everyone's enjoyment of the game.

Here in Moore County we have a wonderful corps of volunteers who are engaged in organized acts of kindness. Yet, many of them go an extra step and do something not in their job description just to make someone else's day a little happier.

the heart you save may be your own *January, 2011*

The last thing I remember before being wheeled into the operating room at St. Joseph Mercy in Ann Arbor, were instructions about a breathing tube and soft restraints.

The next thing was a nurse in the middle of the night, flipping on the bright overhead lights, telling me they could take the tube out now. And remove the restraints.

What tube? What restraints?

Have they already done the surgery? And I made it! Now what?

My throat was so sore I couldn't get my questions out. That's what husbands and daughters are for.

While I was in never-never land, a team of surgeons had cracked open my chest, put my heart on by-pass, and repaired three pretty good size blockages in my cardiac arteries. They also left behind a leg-long scar marking where they'd gone in to retrieve some good arteries. That was 18 years ago this past December. The scars are still there but not quite so ugly and barely visible.

We are constantly being told that women tend not to take care of their hearts. They tend not to listen to what their bodies are trying to tell them. I was exceptionally lucky. I had a wonderful young woman as my primary care physician and when I started mentioning a few symptoms like pain between my shoulder blades while on the treadmill, shortness of breath, etc. She immediately placed a call to a cardiologist and within a week I'd had a heart catheterization where some bright young person makes a small slit in your groin and slips in a catheter and some dye so he/she and you can watch what's going on as the dye heads for the myriad of blood vessels around your heart. I could watch it on TV but in those days I needed my glasses, which they'd taken away from me. I could tell by the expression on the cardiologist's face and the conversation with whoever was watching that they didn't like what they saw.

They explained everything to me—could you absorb the information, lying flat on a cold table, with a tube running up to your heart? When I was more or less coherent, it was all explained to my husband and me. This time it made sense but still didn't sound like how I wanted to spend Christmas week. But it did sound serious and needing to be fixed.

It was fixed and whatever they used to put me back together again must be great stuff to have lasted this long. Now I hear they glue your sternum back together instead of staples. But I couldn't wait for the new developments.

Heart attacks are the leading cause of death for women.

We tend to ignore that chest pain that feels like indigestion. We figure the shortness of breath is because we were carrying too many packages. If something like this happened to a spouse or friend, we'd be after them in a minute to get help.

National Women's Heart Month is in February and you'll be hearing a lot about heart disease, the warning signs, etc. For your own health, and for the peace of mind of those around you, please listen to the information and see your doctor just to be sure.

It just might add at least 18 years to your life.

where

. . . this land *July, 2013*
was made for you and me . . .

The last piece in my mental patchwork quilt of these United States has been added. There was a hole, almost in the middle of my quilt where Kansas belonged. Last month we added Kansas as the 50th state I've visited. This has been a long and quite unplanned journey. I did not set out to see all 50 states but as we continued to travel and visit more and more places, I suddenly realized I hadn't been to Kansas! Watching the "Wizard of Oz" over and over didn't really count.

Which state did I like best? Least? Can't really say as each state has something special and I hope the people living there appreciate what they have. I've seen steel towns that are almost completely deserted; I missed the Cuyahoga River on fire in Cleveland but have seen a renewal in the riverfront area. When we moved to Detroit, we got a sympathy card from a Detroit native. There was no need. Certainly there's a part of that city that we called "the war zone." But there were wonderful medical facilities, fine cultural buildings, and a downtown that is coming to life.

There are many places I enjoy visiting but would not choose to live there: New York City; Washington, D.C.; Los Angeles; New Orleans. However, I didn't think I'd like Cleveland or Detroit but found many good things.

Until you've gone from the craggy shores of Maine to California's redwood forests, to the Florida Keys, to Alaska or to Hawaii, it's hard to realize what a very special country we have, geographically. From the northern tip of the Adirondacks to the southern tip of the Blue Ridge Mountains you marvel at each new vista ahead. From the hills of West Virginia to the endless stretches of farmland in the Midwest, to the wonder of the Great Lakes, to the mountains in the west and then the oceans' coastlines, this land that is ours is a study in contrasts.

We've done these trips over a long period of time. I remember crossing over from Canada to the small town of Ogdensburg, New York when I was about 10 years old. I was so disappointed after crossing the St. Lawrence River and finding that the part of the United States we'd gone to looked just like the land across the river. That happens to be the case along the 5,000 mile unguarded border between our northern neighbors and us. In places without border crossing stations, you can walk from one country to another and not realize you've done it.

We've gone by train, car, plane, RV, boat, ferry, and foot. We've seen mansions, magnificent cathedrals, log cabins, simple homes with people swinging or rocking on their porches. It is astounding the number of post-WWII homes that are still standing. The pride their owners take in them is a real testament. We've also seen litter along beautiful roads, houses that have been neglected, businesses that may have once been pillars of their communities but now are boarded up. On balance, I've seen more good than bad.

As for my must-see recommendations for others:

Niagara Falls: the Canadian side gives you a better view of both sets of falls with that side having a distinct edge at night when the light show is outstanding. I've been there in all seasons and the most impressive is winter when an icy wonderland is formed as water hits the cold air.

The Grand Canyon: it's one of those places that defy accurate description; the scenery changes with the light of day; the depth of the gorge is overwhelming; the length of the canyon is remarkable. While in the neighborhood, be sure to see Bryce National Park with its hundreds of red clay towers that make you think of the stone soldiers in China.

"Old Faithful" at Yellowstone: watching that famous geyser from start to finish is breathtaking. It starts slowly with a little steam escaping, then some water, and each time it appears to dip down, it comes back up higher and louder. The experience lasts about 15-20 minutes and if you miss the whole event it will repeat itself with regularity 24 hours a day, 7 days a week. Park guides have the system figured out and will give you an approximate time for the next eruption; their timing is close to exact.

Muir Woods: just north of San Francisco is the most outstanding park of trees I've ever seen. There is a section called 'The Cathedral' and you do feel as if you're on hallowed ground with huge redwoods as tall pillars that sort of bend toward each other at the top. Sunlight filters through the trees much as light comes through a stained glass window and the silence is a wonderful escape from the hustle and bustle of the coastal highway and the city.

Alaska: Denali National Park with Mt. McKinley; Glacier Bay where icebergs calve off the glacier.

The Rocky Mountains: any place you can see and travel across the various mountain ranges is spectacular. We drove up to the Continental Divide in Colorado where we threw snowballs in mid-June and an hour or so later we were enjoying a meal outside in Aspen. You don't have to be a skier to enjoy the mountains, but skiers do appreciate them more.

On this last trip we met a woman about my age who runs a diner/pizza place. She came to visit with us, wondering where we were from and where we were going. She has one unfilled dream: to walk on a beach at the ocean and collect shells. This was in West Virginia, a neighboring state to Virginia with its beaches (I also pointed out that both North and South Carolina have fabulous beaches.) She probably has never been farther than 50 miles from home in her lifetime. I felt very sad that such a simple dream as gathering shells by the ocean was not likely to happen. I also felt exceptionally lucky to have been to all 50 states.

Woody Guthrie's song was written before Alaska or Hawaii became states or I'm sure he'd have included them.

This land is your land, this land is my land
From California, to the New York Island
From the redwood forest, to the gulf stream waters,
This land was made for you and me.

balloon *October, 2014*

Wow!

"That's about the best way I can describe my recent hot air balloon experience. I'm sure there were many other adjectives that could convey how great the experience was. It was thrilling, breathtaking, heart-stirring, mind-blowing, impressive and much more.

Many have asked if it was what I expected. As I had no specific expectations, it was all I could have hoped for—and I've been hoping for such an experience for more than 50 years. It began in 11th grade when our French literature teacher assigned "Le Tour du Monde en Quatre-vingts Jours" in its 1873 original French. "Around the World in Eighty Days" was quickly translated into English and then became a popular movie in 1956.

As I researched the original book, I discovered that Phileas Fogg did not go by hot air balloon anytime during his voyage. Bummer! Illustrators are responsible for my linking the story to a balloon and adding it to my life (a.k.a. bucket) list. Nonetheless, it was a longtime dream, which came true.

We had a perfect day and perfect ride, starting at 6:30 am in a field near Silk Hope where we met Richard and Lindy Parr, a retired couple who love ballooning. The grass was still damp with dew so the assistants, or chase crew, used a large fan to start inflating the balloon to give it a chance to dry out before it was put to work. The balloon cage measured 42 inches by 48 inches with 20-pound propane cylinders nestled in each corner. We were a cozy threesome—Rick, our balloonist; Diana, our photographer; and me, celebrating a life list event for my 75th birthday.

Calm silence surrounded us as we floated over the countryside, with the trees appearing to be a soft cushion below. I was surprised to see many different varieties of trees. When you see overhead pictures from one of the large balloons taken at golf tournaments, that is exactly what the landscape below looked like. The only noise from us was when Rick fed the flame. Dogs greeted us at various levels of barking; an angry black bull in a small pen made it known that he didn't like where he was; deer dashed for cover below us; a fox, in a different area, was prowling the tree line. We skimmed the tops of some tall pines and have souvenir pinecones from one of them.

Looking from above at how land has been divided was intriguing. We saw how trees have been planted to mark territory, how one large house on a large piece of land often has two or three slightly smaller houses built close by. We surmised that these were parents' or grandparents' homes with lots separated out for the next generations.

I was impressed with a church we went over showing how precisely the tombstones stood in the cemetery at the back of the church. Actually, I was impressed with everything I saw. As it was still early in the day, the morning mist on the horizon kept us from seeing some of the skyline of Chapel Hill or Durham. The mist was much more intriguing than a skyline.

Personal history was made that morning—I was up, dressed, fed and on the road shortly after 5 a.m. I'm not a morning person except in cases of emergency or balloon rides.

And yes, I'd do it again.

when

we the people . . . *July, 2012*

It's time to get out your red, white and blue tableware, put up your flags and get ready to celebrate the Fourth of July. There'll be parades, large and small; concerts; cooking out; fireworks. Scattered throughout the day will be visits with family and friends and enjoying a fine Carolina day.

How many of us will remember that we are celebrating the 236th anniversary of the Declaration of Independence and the wise words contained therein. The thoughtful men who formed the Continental Congress and drew up what we loosely refer to as the Constitution would not likely recognize the country or its people today. Yet, they were able to give us a living document to guide us on our way to independence from Great Britain and begin life as the United States of America.

The Preamble states: "We the people of the United States, in order to form a more perfect Union, establish justice, insure domestic tranquility, provide for the common defence*, promote the general welfare, and secure the blessings of liberty to ourselves and our posterity, do ordain and establish this Constitution for the United States of America."

Great Britain was not in favor of this act and thus began our first war as a nation. Lives were lost on both sides and, for a time, relations were strained after we won. Fortunately all that has improved over the ages and we are now good friends and allies.

After the war, it became apparent to the co-signers of the Constitution that some additions were needed and 10 amendments, commonly referred to as 'The Bill of Rights' were added. Some of these 10 are more widely known than others—the right to freedom of speech, the right to bear arms, the right to not incriminate oneself, the right to a speedy trial.

With each right comes responsibility, although that is not clearly spelled out for us. The fathers of our country assumed that we would recognize that free speech did not give you the right to yell "fire!" in a crowded theater if there was no fire. The right to bear arms does not include the right to drive by and shoot innocent civilians just because you own a gun.

Since the Preamble clearly states that domestic tranquility and general welfare are among the things to be treasured by the new nation, one has to wonder what happened when we see so much domestic warfare and a lack of general welfare. It's very hard to find a newscast that doesn't start with reports of shootings and killings.

Politically we are a country deeply divided. Records of the deliberations by the Continental Congress state that even when the "gentlemen" were seriously at odds over specific points, they were able to come to civil conclusions. That ability has been seriously eroded.

Over the years it became necessary to add amendments to fit the times: slavery was abolished; 'naturalized' citizens were to be given the same rights and responsibilities as those born in the U.S.A.; prohibition was enacted then a few years later abolished. It took wise legislators to realize that wrongs had been done to parts of our country and needed to be repaired.

My favorite amendment is the 19th, which finally granted women the right to vote. Abigail Adams started advocating for women during the first Continental Congress when she advised her husband, John, to "remember the women." It's a shame that neither Adams lived to see women turning out in droves to cast their first ballots.

So, if you get a quiet moment this July Fourth, remember the hard work that has gone into making us a free nation and pledge to help get us back on track to "domestic tranquility."

** defence is not misspelled—that's the British way and was the American way for a while; and, that's a direct quote from the Preamble.*

Countdown *September, 1982*

The back-to-school countdown ends tomorrow for most of us. Some of us began the countdown the minute school was out in June. For others this marks the next step on the road to "growing up."

For some reason, this summer took me a long time to readjust to having another person underfoot. We've both gotten older and perhaps a little more set in our ways. I rather liked my schedule from September through June and then suddenly there was a change. Now that I've more or less adjusted, she's on her way to Fulton Junior High School.

Many years ago I was a teacher in a junior high school. Each September there would be a column in one of our newspapers about the woes of sending children to school for the first time, or back to school, or something along those lines. As a teacher I felt that no one was really paying attention to how we felt that day.

When I switched from classroom to newsroom, I decided to avenge all the "poor parents" and "poor kids" in a September column. But that was before I was a parent, so what did I know?

Now I know.

I have not forsaken my first chosen profession and offer all the teachers who are waiting to greet our children my best wishes for the coming year. I also send some sympathy. Often we parents don't fully appreciate all that teachers do day after day, month after month.

Now that my focus is much more parental, I have some comments for those to whom we are entrusting the education of our children for another year:

Please be patient with them; we haven't quite completed all the finishing touches (will we ever?) but we're still trying. Together we can make it.

Please be firm with them—not nasty, or harsh, or too rigid; just offer a strong, steady firm hand that will guide them. We're not asking you to take over our role as disciplinarian, just to augment it. We'll try to do the same for you.

Please help them to learn life while learning the three "R's"—we'd like to see warm, caring human beings receiving diplomas or passing grades at the end of the year.

Please try to make them responsible citizens. Schools are microcosms of the world and if our children learn how to live cooperatively from nine to three, perhaps that will carry over for the rest of the day and into their lives.

Please forgive us our errors in judgment. Usually we're only thinking of what's best for our children. Sometimes that makes us wear blinders and we may not see the whole picture that you see. Help us understand better what's going into the minds of our children so we can be part of the teaching and learning.

As parents we should pledge to take a more positive interest in our schools. We should be helping our elected board members know how we feel well in advance of their decision making. It's not fair to sit back, do nothing, and then gripe about something we don't like.

While it's hard to do we should be concerned about the welfare of all the children in the school system, not just those whom we are sending. If we pressure for a particular program or subject for our children, who will speak for those whose parents are indifferent to the educational process. "Me first" may work for a while but everyone can't be first.

Good teachers and good administrators are leaving education to go into other fields, which often pay more and offer more self-satisfaction. We need to help these people stay and make our systems better. Sometimes, just a "thanks for a job well done" will make the difference between a teacher realizing that he or she has accomplished something and wondering if what they do matters at all. (That I remember from my days in the classroom—the criticisms come quickly; the congratulations often arrive too little and too late.)

So, it's back to school for all of us. Let's have a good year.

sandwiched *June, 2010*

The 'Sandwich Generation' is not a group of folks who happen to prefer different kinds of sandwiches—PBJ, grilled cheese, panini, pita, etc.

Instead, it's a group of people who find themselves caught between two other generations. Usually, the ones in the middle are trying to meet the needs of those older and younger than they. Sometimes grandparents form the top layer. Sometimes it's parents. Sometimes it might be a person from your extended or blended family. Wherever they fit in the definition, the people in this layer are those who count on you for help. It may be financial assistance, it may be caregiving need, it may be emotional demands.

Those in the middle layer are the sandwich filling, which most of us consider the best part of a sandwich. They are holding the top and bottom layers together. Sometimes this bond is rather loosely constructed. In other cases it's a closely-knit link. The type of connection will determine the action needed.

On the bottom of this generational sandwich are our children or grandchildren. For some people, they have a double portion, caring for both their children and their children's children.

Baby Boomers were the first to really define this phenomenon. Family and friends caring for each other is not a new thing. For centuries, generations have taken care of each other. What makes the difference is that we have changed. Our parents are living longer; we are having children at an older age; grown children are returning home for a roof over their heads and help with life's demands.

A few years ago (or was it decades?) I announced that if this was the sandwich generation, then I must be the peanut butter. I felt as if everything was sticking to me and I had to take care of everyone's needs. My mother was in failing health, my daughter was a teenager. I was a working journalist with regular deadlines that had to be met. I had a husband whose job required a lot of travel time away from home. Juggling various wants and needs was a daily event. And, as in most sandwiched cases, the one in the middle gets squeezed the most.

Personally, most of these demands have now worked themselves out and I survived more or less intact. I learned a great deal from the experience: you can't be all things to all people and hope to maintain a stable, fulfilling life for yourself. On some days, you need to make choices about which need will be taken care of first.

And I've learned that the world does not stop the day you choose your own life as your top priority that day.

When you become overly stressed, you really aren't much help to the other parts of the sandwich. Stress makes us do all sorts of things that we know are not what we really want. Stress contributes to many diseases which might not have come our way otherwise.

"Stop and smell the roses" seems like such a trite, overused phrase, but it has real meaning. No matter which part of the sandwich you are, learn to take time to stop and enjoy.

"Thanks" comes in many forms

November, 2011

At this time of year people are expected to list the many things in their lives for which they are thankful. Taking time to count your blessings is a good thing. I have a long list of things that fill my life with joy and meaning.

Yet, there are many things that I would deeply appreciate:

I'd love to see world peace. I'll settle for respect and civility among those in my neighborhood, my county, my state, my country. We've really gotten way off balance when it comes to treating each other decently. We don't have to agree on everything but the very least we can do is not attack those with whom we don't agree. From politicians to kids on the playground or on Facebook, bullying is no longer acceptable. Neither is lying, stretching the truth, playing "gotcha" with video cameras and publicly embarrassing others for millions to see. Stopping this would make me grateful.

I'd love to see every driver use his or her signal light to give other drivers a clue as to where they are headed. Charles Kuralt once wrote, "You know you're in a small town when the person in front of you doesn't signal and you know where they are going anyway." Whether we live in a small town, on a farm, in a larger town or even a big city, we need to realize that people around you are not mind readers. Give them a hint by using the signal. That would make me grateful.

Cell phones and all the other new electronic gadgets were great inventions. They each have many useful purposes. I don't believe that inventors intended that the use of cell phones in public was meant to let everyone in hearing distance know about a perfect stranger's love life, or grocery list, or mean mother-in-law. I own and use a cell phone but try to do so in a very limited way. Not having to hear conversations that don't affect me would make me very grateful.

Having alleged news commentators interpret what we've just watched and listened to is offensive. We do not need to be told about the hidden meaning behind a major speech. We can see and hear for ourselves. If we didn't get the message as it was delivered, we probably weren't paying attention. We may have been waiting for a 'talking head' to explain it. Taking responsibility for our own thoughts and deeds would make me exceptionally grateful.

The economy has tended to increase tensions. When you don't know if your job will be there tomorrow, or you've already lost your job and have not found one for months, you have a right to be worried about your future. If you have a family to care for, your worries are multiplied. Our many wonderful agencies that help people in need are feeling more than a pinch, they're feeling a huge punch. They are doing more with less and wondering how long they can keep on. Lending a helping hand, no matter how small, can take a little pressure off.

Now, that would make me fantastically grateful.

thanks, dad *June, 1983*

In the interest of total equality and fair play, and because it has been pointed out to me that some of my comments in Mothers' Day columns were somewhat biased against husbands and fathers, I now offer the other side if the coin.

It has been quite a year for things written about men with "Real Men" comments leading the way. You remember them—they don't eat quiche and don't do a lot of other things considered suitable for wimps. Just when we were getting used to new, shared responsibilities some wimp comes along and tries to tell us what "Real Men" ought to do. Now there's a "Real Women" handbook, which proves that one good commercial idea spawns at least three more.

No offense was meant by my "Where is it Written" column. But, since I did hear from a number of irate male readers, one who attempts to share my life, I offer, not an apology, but some words of appreciation for husbands and fathers:

> For doing the dishes when you know we've had a rotten day, we thank you.
>
> For helping around the house which includes everything from killing the spider hovering over the bed to arranging, re-arranging, then arranging again the living room furniture, we thank you.'
>
> For not saying "I told you so" when you did say the gas gauge was registering below empty and you had to come to our rescue, we thank you.

For taking an interest in our day, whether it was exciting or boring, we thank you.

For caring about the kids and helping them with homework and playtime, we thank you.

For changing messy diapers and cleaning up after sick kids, we thank you.

For trying to understand that our minds and yours work differently, even though you may never fully grasp the concept, we thank you.

For appreciating the fact that we can balance a checkbook as well as a meal, we thank you.

For not calling us "the wife," "the little lady," "the old lady," we thank you.

For letting us know that while we appreciate your strengths you feel safe enough to let us share your weaknesses, we thank you.

For trying to do some of these things some of the time, we thank you.

Fruitcakes *November, 2000*

On Thanksgiving Day I prepared to tackle THE Christmas Fruitcake.

It's a process that can take two or three days depending on family schedules, commitments, etc. The family, or part thereof that lives near the baker, has to be present together for at least a few minutes so that each can stir the contents. I have decided that stirring the mound of fruit is sufficient to fulfill my mother's long-held belief that we all have to stir it so we'll have a good year.

In the past few years I've been somewhat remiss in fruitcake duty. I actually missed one year. Then, last year, I opted to do my mother-in-law's recipe, which is quite different. Don't ask me to choose which is better. They are both good and we happen to like fruitcake.

Christmas fruitcakes get a bad rap. Jokes abound making fun of passing one leaden cake around the family year after year, hoping no one will notice that you didn't eat it. Obviously, these comedians have never made a fruitcake, nor have they tasted any from my family.

How could you not love something that has butter (real), eggs (real), fruit, dark brown sugar, flour, lemon juice, strong coffee, and with some alcohol if that's your taste. You have no heart if the scent of the baking cake doesn't bring you to the kitchen in hopes of either getting to "lick the bowl" or grab a few crumbs.

I marvel at my mother's generation for the effort they made for these cakes, and everything else they made from scratch. The first year I took over this duty, my mother was recovering from foot surgery and was staying with us. Somewhat reluctantly she passed the baton but watched very carefully as I did each step.

My kitchen was a modern one with lots of timesaving appliances. I could chop nuts in a few seconds in my food processor whereas she'd done them by hand. I have a strange looking gadget to separate egg yolks from the whites but she had to use a steady hand and use the cracked shell carefully to do this. We both have juice squeezers to get the juice and not the seeds.

I have a whisk to fluff the egg whites, she worked with a fork. I creamed the sugar and butter with an electric mixer then added all the other stuff, in specific order, and kept using the mixer. She used a wooden spoon from start to finish and was appalled that I chose a strong plastic spoon and spatula for mixing. My oven stays at whatever temperature I set and I can use the built-in timer to remind to check on what's going on inside.

Her yellowing recipe card suggests baking at a medium heat for three to four hours. She tested doneness with a straw from the kitchen broom. My cakes take about two hours, and my tester is a piece of thin spaghetti.

When it became clear to her that I could handle this annual chore, she handed over a set of four tins that have seen more Christmases than I. Most years, my cakes have been almost as good as hers.

The next time you deride a fruitcake, think of what my mother and I (and hundreds like us) have gone through to keep up this tradition.

chanukah *December, 1975*

The Jewish feast of Chanukah is a "happy time" according to Chuck Lipsig, young son of Joe and Bobby Lipsig of Oswego.

On the final day of the eight-day celebration, I chatted with Chuck as he explained the significance of Chanukah and lit the traditional candelabra, the menorah, for me. As it was the last evening of the feast, most of the candles were already burning. Beginning on the first day a candle is lit every day. On the eighth day the last candle is lit. Chuck, wearing his yarmulke, sang a Hebrew song as he set the candle aflame.

He explained that Chanukah is a thanksgiving observance. It dates back to 165 BC when the Jews in Judea defeated the Syrian tyrant Antiochus IV after a three-year struggle. They held celebrations in the temple in Jerusalem and rededicated it to God. After clearing the temple of Syrian idols, they found only one small container of oil with which to light their holy lamps. Miraculously, the oil lasted for eight days. Judas Macabaeus, the Jewish leader, then proclaimed the Chanukah festival to be observed henceforth. Chanukah is often referred to as the "Festival of Lights."

The Jewish tradition of serving potato pancakes, latkes, has an interesting origin. Chuck noted that during the hostilities between the Hebrews and the Syrians, the Hebrew women made latkes heavily laden with salt and fed them to the enemy. The salt made them thirsty so the women gave them wine. The latkes-wine-latkes-wine cycle was repeated until the Syrians were in a drunken stupor and were overtaken by the Hebrews. Chuck was quick to point out that today's latkes are not heavily salted.

Each evening when the menorah is lit gifts are exchanged—mostly children are the recipients. A traditional gift is a top or dreidel, which has special significance. While under Syrian rule, the Jewish people were not allowed to study the Torah but were allowed to gamble. They managed to secretly study their sacred book while having a lookout watch for Syrians. Then the Torah was hidden and the dreidels appeared giving the cover of innocent gambling. Chuck showed me his favorite dreidel, a shiny silver one with Hebrew letters on it.

The Chanukah holiday begins on the 25th day of the month of Kislev in the Hebrew calendar and lasts eight days.

Our Christmas Tree *December, 2000*

Martha Stewart probably wouldn't approve of our Christmas tree. The Festival of Trees people aren't likely to beat a path to my door seeking my expertly decorated tree. But anyone interested in a slice of pop culture or some family history during the past three decades may find it interesting. As for me and mine, we find it suits our needs just fine.

Decorating the tree can be a nostalgic trip down memory lane. At one time, before children, I usually followed a simple theme with coordinating lights and balls. Every now and then I think a "theme" tree might be worth trying—I'd use white silk magnolias and filmy gold ribbon and nothing else. It might be very pretty but it certainly wouldn't remind me of the many years we've been doing this, and how, after a child enters your life, you see things differently.

I'd miss all those ornaments that have dates to mark the passing of time. The cute little wooden rocking horse we got when Beth was a baby or the adorable brass little girl holding a bell.

There are many handmade ornaments from friends. Three sleeping felt mice tucked into walnut shell beds were given to us in 1972, and each year I wonder if they've survived another year in storage. They have a central spot this year. Close to them are two skiers and one person in a sled, handmade in minute detail by a Norwegian foreign student who lived with us for almost a year. The sled was made especially for me, the non-skier.

There are three china bells with shamrocks brought back from Ireland in 1980 and not far away a lovely Belleek china shamrock from another trip. Most of the annual ornaments are traditional round ones and reflect what was going on in our lives—Sesame Street kids from 1974, Snoopy and friends a year later, a Hummel angel marking a trip to Germany, a crystal teddy bear with cloves fashioned into flowers found in a small Yule market in Austria, Santa with an Olympic torch for 1980 when we went to the Winter Olympics in Lake Placid, another Santa playing soccer to remember our experience with World Cup Soccer in Detroit in 1994. There's even a miniature outhouse, decorated for Christmas, to remind my husband of successful participation in an outhouse race during the annual tobacco festival in a little town in Kentucky. (I usually place that ornament near the back of the tree.)

We have a wooden Santa that says "Mele Kalikamakau" from our first trip to our 50th state. Alaska is represented by a Christmas moose on white china. Canada is seen in a gold maple leaf, which was a gift, and in an Eskimo hockey player. A multi-colored small sequined wreath came from Hong Kong.

An angel handkerchief doll fashioned after the Civil War sits on the top. She has companions sprinkled throughout including a stained glass angel made by a young Beth. There's a cat angel, and a nice plump angel that perches on one of the branches.

The "Twelve Days of Christmas" gold ornaments are the only ones I insist on putting on in order. We do try to organize the yearly treasures somewhat. My right-handed engineer likes to have symmetry in the tree and we usually agree. The lowest branches are pretty bare save for a few unbreakable ornaments to keep our cat from systematically dismantling our treasures.

So, Martha, I make no apologies for our very personal tree.

things that go bump in the night . . .

November, 2012

It's that time of year when we begin to think about people and things that we are grateful to have in our lives.

This year I am exceptionally thankful for many things, mostly that I'm still able to walk and talk and write this column. Almost a year ago I had a really bad fall in the middle of the night and bounced my head several times against the side of a solid cherry dresser. It was quite a shock—at first I thought I'd broken my shoulder, then my legs wouldn't work and finally came the headache. My husband had to help me up and after a few minutes I realized that other than a few bumps, bruises and muscle strains, I was still in one piece. So I took something for my headache and went back to bed. (Of course, had that been my daughter, or someone else, I would have known not to let her sleep nor have medication.)

The next week is a blur. There were a number of social functions that we had agreed to attend and I could rest in the afternoon then put on my party self and go out. On about the eighth day a very observant friend took me aside, looked me in the eyes and asked what was wrong. I guess my speech pattern, my gait, and my eyes didn't look right. The next day my acupuncturist, Lance Allen, said basically the same and noted a few more abnormalities. When he said he would not work on me until I'd had a CAT scan, that got my attention.

My family doctor arranged for the CAT scan and a referral to a neurologist who tested my mind and arranged for an MRI. Everything was more or less normal. I had "post concussive syndrome." Only rest and no stress will help my brain heal and it could take up to a year. I immediately went to the Mayo Clinic webpage for more information on this syndrome and, sure enough, I had all but one of the symptoms, and it gave the same recommendation of rest and no stress.

There were many days when I felt that someone had pumped cotton candy into my brain. But there were other days when I felt clearer-headed. Memory has been a problem and I think there's a good chance that some things may not return. A few months later I did win a game of Trivial Pursuit against my thirty-something nephew who is very good at the game. That gave me great hope, even if he might have let me win.

A strange side effect was difficulty working with numbers in any sort of line or grid arrangement. I could tell a bridge score but I couldn't write the information in the right places; tax time was a nightmare and I had to stop my usual task of getting the yearly information organized.

I felt somewhat encouraged when I read of hockey and football players having "post concussive syndrome." I wasn't glad they had it but I was relieved to know it was a real thing. After another fall and real bang on my head from hitting an open cupboard door, Dr. Solomon suggested maybe I needed a helmet. There's an old hockey helmet in the garage if I need it.

I'm doing much better and can now recognize the signs of fogginess coming and stop what I'm doing. I think there will be some permanent glitches but, compared to what head injuries do to lots of folks, I am grateful.

The one thing that seemed to remain intact was being able to write. Our editor, Carrie Frye, and her assistant, Jessica Bricker, were wonderful to me and for that I am grateful.

Lance Allen and Dr. Bruce Solomon were caring and careful and for that I am grateful.

Friends and family, particularly my husband and daughter, were patient and understanding and just let me heal and for that I am over-the-top grateful.

goodbye *July, 1983*

Fourteen years ago this week, two weary travelers arrived in Oswego after a long, hot journey from West Virginia. One of us came because of a job transfer at Alcan and the other came along as a rather dutiful wife.

We arrived on a Sunday night at the Pontiac Hotel and bright and early Monday morning city crews began work on what is now the west side parking lot, right below our window. "Welcome to Oswego," I thought as I realized my plan for a nice long sleep-in that day and every day in the summer had just been shattered by workmen's drills. Other digging would follow; then the leveling of the lot to hold the black, smelly asphalt. This was not the summer on Lake Ontario that I had counted on.

Before long we found a house that was to become our home in Bundyville and began to settle in to a new life. In time we met some wonderful people, some of whom we are leaving behind. We were blessed with wonderful neighbors.

Although we came as foreigners, we are leaving as American citizens and we have added an honest-to-gosh Oswegonian to our family. She came into the world in the Oswego Hospital in 1970.

The first person to give me a chance to get into print here was George Caruso of the Oswego Shopper. I remain grateful for that start. The person who helped me adjust to the pressure of reporting for a daily paper was Jack Wood, former Oswego bureau chief for the Syracuse Newspapers. Working with Jack was a real adventure and I know I couldn't even think about daily newspaper work if it weren't for Jack.

The last group of people with whom I'm working is an incredible bunch. The reading public has no idea of the amount of time, hard work and downright dedication of the Oswego County Messenger staff. They have taught me that getting the story and getting it right is not only important but a must.

To all the people, both in public and private life, who have helped me get a story, a very special thanks. Whether you were the object of a feature story, the subject of a news story, or a reliable source that we reporters could not live without, thank you for your faith and trust that I would do you and your story justice.

As we three prepare to leave, there is much we shall miss—the river on whose banks we live, the lake which joins this country with our native country, the famous sunsets, the magnificent historical buildings and homes, the potential for a booming waterfront.

Of course there are a few things we shall not miss—being snowed in, common council bickering and some foolish things done in the name of politics.

Sometimes it takes an outsider to recognize the possibilities that are open to any community. We see great potential here and would like to stay and help bring some of the projects we worked on to fruition. We are grateful for the Oswego experience in our lives—it has been about one-third of our lives, more than half of our married life and all of our daughter's life.

Since our move to Cleveland, Ohio was announced, I've been putting it off in my mind. I've also been saying, "I never say goodbye" because it sounds so final. My hairdresser even had those words on a cake for me at my last appointment.

After two years in Cleveland, we moved to Russellville, Kentucky for five years, then back to Kingston, Ontario for two years, then on to Detroit, Michigan for five years and, in 1997, an early retirement to Whispering Pines, North Carolina.

why

Married is Better *August, 2010*

More than 40 years ago one of my favorite poets, Judith Viorst, wrote "Married is Better." At the time I totally agreed with her, and still do.

Late last month we celebrated our 50th wedding anniversary. Fifty years with the same person! It's truly hard to imagine where those five decades have gone. After all we're still basically the same fun-loving kids we were in 1960, aren't we?

Who knew then that we would leave our native land, legally live in five states and become U.S citizens? Who knew that he would have to travel a great deal and I would often get to go along to foreign lands?

We've learned a lot in 50 years. As the oldest children in both our families, we've learned the need to do what we can for our parents, grandparents, aunts and uncles. Family comes first. Running a very close second are friends. When you move away from where you grew up, friends quickly become your social glue. We have been exceptionally lucky and still have good friends both in Canada and the states where we lived. Retirement has enlarged and enhanced our circle of friends—most of us don't have our families just down the road a bit, or in the next town, not even in the next state, so we fill those empty family spots with good friends.

I'm not sure that you'd consider us a "perfect match." Nothing is perfect. But somehow we muddled through and got to this landmark anniversary.

He's a right-handed engineer, born under the orderly sign of Virgo. I'm a left-handed klutz, born under Leo's more flamboyant sign. *Married is better.*

He's an outdoorsman who likes almost any sport out there, whether as a player or spectator. I'm more of the indoor type. He brings home the news from the golf course. I bring the gossip from the bridge table. *Married is better.*

When he mangled his shoulder and several adjoining parts in a ski accident, I quickly learned to be a caregiver, and depending on the day, a drill sergeant, more of a nag, or a compassionate companion. When I broke my left arm, was casted from shoulder to fingertips and was helpless, our roles were reversed. *Married is better.*

I cry at sad movies. I cry at happy movies. I can even shed a few tears at a commercial. He hands me his handkerchief. *Married is better.*

As we age and have annoying things like doctors' appointments, 'procedures,' therapy with aches and pains, it's so good to have someone to lean on, to do the driving, to talk back to the medical profession when needed. *Married is better.*

With very little guidance, he can shop for groceries and then cook them. *Married is better.*

We have one daughter who has brought much joy and happiness, tears and laughter, adventure and bravado, surprises and challenges to 40 of these 50 years. *Married is better.*

When we got married, we never thought about a 50th anniversary. In those days, people who made it to 25 years were special—and *old*, like our parents. Now we read about lots of 50s, several 60s, and even a few 70s in years together.

Married is definitely better.

maintenance *January, 2002*

Have you noticed that general maintenance seems to take longer with age?

Gone are the days of splashing some soap and water on your face at night, brushing your teeth, and climbing into bed. No more dashing out of bed in the morning, grabbing a quick shower, throwing on the right clothes and charging out the door ready to take on the world.

I *know* I used to do that. It seems like it wasn't that long ago. But no more.

Although I am not now, nor ever have been, nor am ever likely to be a slave to fashion and cosmetics, I do take much longer to get ready for the day and to undo whatever the day did to me. Splashing cold water on my face still helps me wake up but that's just the beginning. As I look blearily into the mirror and see a fuzzy image of a much older person staring back, I realize I need my glasses. But they serve only to bring into focus the things that need to be done before I can show my face outside the house.

Before starting the shower, I need to decide what's on the agenda for the day and therefore what clothes to consider. Perhaps I'll even have to set up the ironing board if I really want to look presentable. I don't do well with decisions first thing—and, truth be told, by the time I'm considering a shower; it's not the first thing in the morning. I've already had breakfast, read the paper, and watched CNN to see if the world blew apart overnight.

Taking a shower used to be a simple in-and-out thing. Now some of my aches enjoy soaking in the warm flow of water and I stand there in a semi-trance with my mind wandering. Skin care is now a more serious problem so I have to gently wash off the night's sleep and hope the creases made by the pillow will be gone from my face. There's not much I can do about the other creases in my skin. Reaching to make sure all body parts get clean takes longer. I hold on to the handicap bar, which I insisted upon when we built the house, saying, "I'm only going to get older here." That requires one hand. Applying soap to a washcloth isn't easy with one hand so some geriatric dexterity comes into play. I look at my feet and wonder how I can best get them clean without getting my head wet from the shower's flow. If I'm in a hurry, I hope that the soapy water running down from the rest of my body will magically clean those feet.

Even getting toweled off takes time. My arms don't swing around quite the way they once did. It takes more effort to lift my legs so I can reach my feet. Next there's the ritual of deodorant, powder, lotion for some places, cream for others. It takes more lotion and cream to make my skin feel soft—probably the extra creases are absorbing more.

Now I'm ready for the sunscreen foundation lotion, perhaps a touch of makeup, also with sunscreen and then some extra color for my cheeks since the sunscreen does its job so well I don't have a lot of natural rosy blush. Hair that once fell into place with a quick shake of my head now needs to be coaxed and carefully arranged and then almost glued in place.

And to think that in 12 hours or so, I reverse the procedure and apply night cleansers and moisturizers that promise to help me retain that youthful glow. Ha!

loss *September, 2000*

The loss of a parent is one of life's landmarks that we'd like to avoid. But when that parent has lived a long, full life and her quality of life has been deteriorating, it's time to let go.

My mother died a few weeks ago at the age of 91. I think she was more than ready to be released and to join my father who died 22 years ago.

As much as you know the inevitable is approaching, the final truth is still a shock. My brother had called the night before to say he thought she was near the end of her downward struggle. His call helped us start to physically prepare for the trip home. When he called the next morning to say her battle was over, we were relieved for her and sad for us.

My mother was the ninth of 10 children to die. She is survived by an older sister. She leaves behind my brother and me, our spouses and four grandchildren. She was born Kathleen May O'Meara; her parents were Elizabeth Finnerty and William O'Meara. She married Patrick Earl Murphy. She was proud of her Irish heritage and when we gave her first granddaughter on St. Patrick's Day in 1970 it seemed like more than a little luck of the Irish.

Being a loving wife and mother was the job she was meant to have. And we have benefited from this. My brother and I went to school within walking distance of our home. On cold winter mornings she would place our coats, snowpants, mitts and galoshes close to the furnace vent to warm them for us. At noon we came home for hot homemade soup simmering on the back of the stove. After school she was waiting for us with a snack.

We grew up just before television—it arrived when I was in high school. Radio was the main source of outside entertainment but we had lots of things to do on our own. Playing cards was major pastime. My mother would happily sit with us and our friends on a rainy summer afternoon and play *Old Maid* or *Go Fish* for hours. It was a pastime she continued with her grandchildren.

My nephew, Tom, fondly remembered time spent with Nana in his touching, sometimes humorous, eulogy on behalf of the grandchildren. Her two granddaughters did the readings during the funeral Mass, and I did a brief eulogy, which included an invitation to an Irish wake. You don't have to be Irish to attend one of these celebrations of life, but it does help you to understand the profound importance of such events. Wonderful family stories are told and, in the telling, are thus passed to the next generation. Usually some great music is playing. We all felt that my mother was enjoying her wake.

She had a ready smile, a great sense of humor, fierce loyalty to her family, her church, and her political party. There were times when she felt each of us in our turn could walk on water and wasn't shy about telling others about her family. And there were other times when each of us felt her Irish temper when we had done something less than was expected.

I feel a peace for and about her now. She is definitely in a much better place. I know we'll hear from her in good times and bad ahead. We all have another angel watching out for us. We'll try not to let her down.

"…and, until we meet again, may God hold you in the palm of his hand."—Irish Blessing

lrn'n sumthin new *September, 2000*

Remember when "LOL" at the end of a note meant "lots of love"?

Not anymore. In today's world of texts and tweets, LOL means "laughing out loud."

At first I strongly objected to changing the meaning of a long used acronym. I would prefer to think that someone sending me a message was closing with 'love' instead of 'laughing.'

As a wordsmith, I am in favor of using real words, properly spelled, in the correct context. But as a mother who wants to stay in touch with her daughter, I need to update (or possibly downgrade) my vocabulary. The "largest list of chat acronyms and text message shorthand" can be found at www.netlingo.com. There are 2052 acronyms out there! Some cannot be printed in this magazine and should probably be banned, but that would be censorship, and if we believe in a free press then we have to live and let live.

I find I am learning to appreciate texting. It conveys a message without interrupting the receiver. It permits an answer at a time convenient to the recipient. I often forget that not everyone is retired and needs to work to put food on the table and keep a roof over their heads. So I try not to interrupt during normal business hours. (Although, there are many of us retired folk who lead pretty busy lives and sometimes are difficult to contact.)

I did find a couple of alternatives to LOL. One was LYL or "love you lots." The other, mostly for seniors was "living on Lipitor.'

A friend sent me a list of acronyms designed especially for seniors, with the recommendation that we pass the list on to children and grandchildren so they'll know what we're trying to tell them. It's called the STC, senior texting code, and says if you qualify for senior discounts, then this code is for you:

> ATD—at the doctor's; BFF—best friend fainted; BTW—bring the wheelchair; BYOT—bring your own teeth; CBM—covered by Medicare; CGU—can't get up; CUATSC—see you at the Senior Center; DWI—driving while incontinent; FWB—friend with beta blockers; FWIW—forgot where I was; FYI—found your insulin; GGPBL—got to go, pacemaker battery low; GHA—got heartburn again; IMHO—is my hearing aid on? LMDO—laughing my dentures out.

For communicating with others there are many more shortcuts:

> ACORN—completely obsessive really nutty person; AEAP—as early as possible; AGB—almost good bridge; AGKWE—and God Knows what else; ALOL—actually laughing out loud; AWHFY—are we having fun yet; BCNU—be seeing you.

I love these three: BFF, BFFN, and BFFTTE. First is Best Friends Forever; next means Best Friends for Now; and the last one is Best Friends Forever Til The End.

> I thought best friend meant exactly that but
> now you have options, which beg the
> question who really is the best friend.

As I read the long list, some of it started to make sense. I recall a period in public schools where spelling was almost optional in the beginning grades where children were encouraged to write what they thought the word sounded like. It was an experiment that didn't succeed then but has come back to haunt us with the shortcuts to texting and tweeting. The reason for this use of the language is, of course, computers. You are allowed a limited number of characters per message. Writing full and complete words would lengthen your text considerably. So someone came up with a way to short-circuit the system. I can't help but feel that that individual was part of failed spelling experiment.

aging

March, 2000

I am increasingly aware that all things were not created equal when it comes to "seniors."

First, the age at which one officially becomes senior varies from 50 to 65.

Once you've had your 50th birthday, you're eligible for membership in the American Association of Retired Persons (AARP). When I got my invitation to join just after that significant birthday, I did not accept. I was insulted. I shouldn't have been, but I was. I didn't realize what a worthwhile organization AARP is, let alone all the great discounts that accompany membership. I am now a card-carrying member.

It seems rather obvious that a person at 50 and one at 70 do not fit a narrow stereotype. We all know 50-somethings who are already old and 70-somethings who will never be old. Society would never treat a baby and a 20-year-old the same way yet it seems willing and anxious to lump anyone approaching 60 together with everyone older than they.

There are a few areas where the stereotype is painfully evident. One is in the advertising world, which caters to the youth image, no matter the product. I thought we'd gotten rid of the "can't trust anyone over 30" myth years ago. How many people over 30 do you see in TV commercials, magazine or newspaper ads? About the only time you see an "older" model is when a product perhaps needed by older people is used, such as denture cleaners, laxatives, disposable undergarments, or insurance.

Someone forgot to inform the Madison Avenue advertising agencies that we "older folks" have the greater percentage of disposable income. We buy many different things. Sometimes we even buy expensive, fun things. We also buy boring things like laundry detergent, pet food, deodorant, floor wax, and paper towels. When was the last time you saw a gray-haired 65-year-old woman cruising down the highway in a sporty car in a television commercial? Or a man with thinning hair playing a computer game without the assistance of his grandchild? Or a cat-lover in orthopedic shoes and sensible clothing feeding an adoring pet?

The point is painfully obvious: age does not fit neatly into one box at 40 and another at 60 and yet another at 80. As alleged seniors, we no more want to be considered as a stereotyped group than a group of teenagers do.

Another area recently occurred to me during a discussion about The Senior Enrichment Center to be built in the county, for the county. The word "senior" appears to distract the attention of those not yet "senior". They will be seniors before they know it. They should realize the importance of an enrichment center for the people of the county, not just a segment of the population about whom they know very little. I have discussed the center casually with people I know and not many of them were aware of the potential for such a place.

If we were trying to build a child care facility of the first order, should only those with children requiring care be interested? What about the Boys' and Girls' Club? It will benefit an age-specific group but people of all ages recognize the importance of such a club. Thus, a senior center should be considered a major asset for a community, not just a place where aging seniors can go to do whatever it is we think seniors do.

This may come as a shock to some, but seniors can do almost anything they want to! Aging bodies are not all inhabited by aging minds. Next time you see a senior citizen, look them in the eyes and you'll be delighted to find there's still plenty of light there.

celebrate aging! *August, 2014*

A great deal is made about getting older—most of it negative. Adding days and years, even minutes and hours is something to be celebrated. This month my minutes, hours and days are adding up to 75 years. 75? How did I get here? I guess I did it just like everyone else—one day at a time.

I certainly have never given much thought to reaching any given age. When you're 16, life is a banquet waiting for you. When you're 21, you've had a small taste of that banquet called life and can hardly wait to see what lies ahead. Then suddenly you're looking at 75! Where did the time go? What have I done with all those minutes and hours? I know enough not to wonder what's ahead.

There are a few other things I know now that I didn't back at 21. A loving family is better than gold. Coming a close second are loving friends, both old and new. Friends help fill in the spaces in life when you no longer live geographically close to family. As we have moved around we've added to our blessings with friends from Fairmont, West Virginia; Oswego, New York; Cleveland, Ohio; Kentucky; Detroit and now North Carolina.

I've learned to never say "never." Then I learned to never say goodbye. My family says I always want the last word and yes, I do. Not in an argument (although that's OK too) but in conversations. I'm pretty sure I can trace that trait to good old-fashioned Irish stubbornness. Over the years I've gathered a lot of stories and tend to use them to make a point. I've done a lot of community work for a good majority of these 75 years thus many interesting tales have attached themselves to my repertoire. One sign of my age might be that I sometimes can't remember the participants in a story or where it happened. Years ago I heard an older woman say, "Oh, my mind must be full" when she forgot something. I have borrowed her phrase many times.

I've learned that forgiveness and second, third or even tenth chances must be part of life. Carrying grudges is a heavy task; so let's let them go.

I've learned that real people appreciate you for who you are, not what you have or what you can do for them. I've also learned that real people are sincere, kind and caring and I'm lucky to know them. As for pretend people, we are not really in the same universe.

I know that I've had a very good life and express gratitude daily. That does not make me blind to those who are struggling, although one dear friend keeps telling me that I can't fix the world. Maybe not, but I can keep trying.

I'm particularly grateful to still have a writing career. When I thought I might be put out to pasture, Carrie Frye came along. I may be the token "older" person at the magazine but it's great fun to be part of a bright, young and talented bunch.

My only brother, younger of course, tells me each year to "consider the alternative" to having a birthday. He means well.

A good friend gave me words for us all to live by: *It's not how old you are; it's how you are old.*

So let the celebration begin!

FINIS

acknowledgments

Diana Mathews, photography
Pat Watterworth, proofreading
Carrie Frye, introduction
Karen Mireau, literary midwife
The Oswego Shopper
Syracuse Post Standard
Oswego Valley News
Oswego Messenger
The Pilot, Southern Pines
OutreachNC, Southern Pines

All the readers through the years
who gave me compliments, criticism and encouragement.
Without a reader, a writer is quite alone.

about the author

Photo by Diana Matthews

Ann Robson has had an eclectic, far-flung journey as a writer, editor, columnist and photojournalist—sparked, as she puts it, by her Irish "luck and pluck."

Ann immigrated to the U.S.A. from Ottawa, Canada in 1968, where she taught English and Science to middle grade students. In upstate New York, she began writing for local papers, which honed her already-keen powers of observation and allowed her to indulge her natural curiosity about her community—especially the often-humorous behavior of her fellow human beings.

After moves to Ohio, Kentucky and Michigan, she became Adjunct Professor of Canadian studies at Western Kentucky University, helping to create the Center for Robert Penn Warren Studies.

Ann's natural funny bone served her well in the course of her teaching and writing life. Early on, she developed a special affinity for the elderly in her community and began volunteering and working on their behalf. She is a dedicated liberal and humanist, who is never afraid to speak out for the underserved.

After moving to North Carolina in 1997, her interest in aging, caregiving and end-of-life-issues led to interaction with many local committees and organizations as well as awards for volunteering and writing on aging issues. She has been involved with the RSVP (Retired Seniors Volunteer Program) of Moore County Department of Aging since 2003 and served as Senior Leader at UNC Institute on Aging, where she authored *Hand to Hand: A Practical Guide for Caregivers.*

Ann continues to work, write, laugh and wonder what the heck this life is all about. She lives with her husband, Bruce, in Whispering Pines, North Carolina. She has worked for The Pilot newspaper and for five years wrote a column on aging for OutreachNC magazine.

This is her first collection of creative nonfiction.

This book of essays by Ann Robson
may be ordered directly at www.lulu.com.

Learn more at:
http://overmyshoulder.blogspot.com

azaleaartpress.blogspot.com

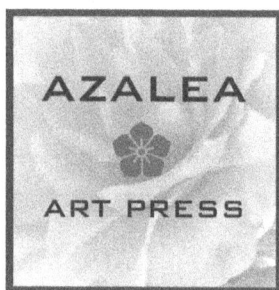

AZALEA
ART PRESS

Azalea.Art.Press@gmail.com

Please contact the author directly at
overmyshoulder@charter.net

To schedule an interview or signing with the
author, please contact the publisher.

www.ingramcontent.com/pod-product-compliance
Lightning Source LLC
Chambersburg PA
CBHW021009090426
42738CB00007B/720
9781943471034